The Day My Dad Came Home

Home

VOLUME ONE

———

Jennifer Crenshaw

THE DAY MY DAD CAME HOME

VOLUME ONE

ISBN (978-1-63944837-1)

Dedication

I would like to dedicate this book to My dad Bobby Crenshaw and My Stepmother, Betty Simmons, and finally Kelvin Hawkins. We have all endured so much since the beginning of this never-ending cycle of violence, drama, evil, and despair, but God is and will always prevail against the evil we can see and those we cannot.

Dad, I love you and forgive you for all things. All I ever wanted was for you to be happy and treated with the dignity and respect you deserved. You deserved to have free will to love who you chose to love. You also deserved peace in your home and your life, and as your daughter, I was going to make sure that happened and you were safe by any means necessary. Dad, I will forever be your right-hand man, and we will get through anything if we stick together. Live your life; you deserve it, and more. I love you, Infinity.

As I wrote this book, Betty Simmons, Ma Betty, we lost you, and I will never be the same. I will always feel that your sickness and death were precipitated by evil, and no one can convince me otherwise but, know I had your back as much as I had my dad's back. In the end, the person responsible for it all will have to answer to a higher power for all the evil, deaths, and pain she has caused. I am my father's keeper, and I will remain vigilant and prepared to always fight for him and even you, no matter what. Thanks for always being my mom; I will never let you go. RIP, I will always love you.

Kelvin Hawkins, you are the love of my life and I thank you and appreciate you for standing by me during a time when you never knew what was going on with me. You were the first to love me during a time when others wouldn't even look at me and the love we shared meant the world to me. You loved me when I didn't even know who I was and could not explain to you what was happening to me. When you left, my world changed forever, and I pray that one day we will continue to fulfill our dreams and our love forever. I also want you to know that you were not responsible, and I forgive you and will never hold you accountable for anything that transpired during our relationship. Thank God for healing and you.

I love you forever, KeJe!

Table of Contents

Foreword

It is my pleasure to know Jennifer C. Sherman. We went to school in the same county for about a year, and she moved away. The Social Media Platform Facebook allowed us to reconnect after over more than twenty years. Many of the occurrences you are about to read about, Jen would call me on the way to the location and ask me to be in prayer with her concerning matters.

I admire Jen for coming forth to write this book because I believe it will bring closure to commence the healing that she will have after the writing process.

- Alfreda Hatcher

From the very beginning of this storm, we have discussed the whys and what for's. I expressed to many who found this situation unreal, but I have always said that if you believe in God, you have to believe in the devil. Only your faith has given you the power to not be defeated!! The Sidechick never knew what the devil was leading her to. But God led you to victory! Love you, girl! Proceed!!!!

- Sharon Evans

I have lived through this nightmare with my best friend, Jen. I have seen the evidence, felt her pain, and witnessed her strength to fight back. Even though she is still living this nightmare, she chooses to share her truth with the world! She is courageous, a true friend, and a woman of substance! As Jen continues her journey, I will forever stand by her side! Fighting the war of WITCHCRAFT!

-   Betty Burnett

Preface

The Day My Dad Came Home – Book One is about my father's mentally ill Sidechick – a sadistic, evil, black-hearted, desperate, and insecure woman who felt she needed to put roots on my father to take him away from my Stepmom and me. And I stopped her dead in her tracks.

When I was sentenced in the Mcduffie County Court system as a convicted felon under the First Offenders Act, on September 20, 2021, for ¼ counts for standing up to the damage of property and the threats made by this desperate, psychotic bully. I knew I had been railroaded by the legal system and the Mcduffie County District Attorney's Office. I was the victim with police reports in hand to prove it. But, repeatedly, no one would listen to me. After experiencing a no-win situation, I felt the need to tell my story and speak my truth about what this woman did to me and my father just to gain his love. I have never experienced in my life a woman who was so desperate for love that she would alter someone's free will to make them love her.

But that's just what she did and almost succeeded until I came home. She expected Main Chick privileges while carrying a Sidechick Label, and I got in her way, and for that, I must pay with my life, or at least that is what she thought.

Sidechick, you lose!

Introduction

The purpose and goal of this book is to help anyone who may
be experiencing unexplainable things repeatedly that are
occurring to you without explanation. What My Father, I, and my
family, among others, endured at the hands of witchcraft, and
although I do not practice nor condone anything related to the
topic of my book, by default, I am now fully experienced in the
Spirit world and how desperate and evil some people can be in
order to get the things they cannot have. This is a place I never
wanted to be. I will forever be thankful for God placing the right
people at the right time in my life to explain what I was
experiencing and help me to fight the devil because I could not
have done it alone. I am sure with the completion of reading my
book. This book will give clarity and the answers to all the
questions that people have experienced similar things and did not
understand. I pray for all that you never go through what I and
my father went through during this time. But, if I can help one
person to seek help outside of the natural realm and gain peace
through healing and understanding, and finally freedom, I have
fulfilled my purpose.

Chapter One

The Introduction

"On the first day I met her in 2013, I was shocked. My Dad normally liked petite women, yet the thicker the women, the more the jokes. So, I adapted to yet another woman. My favorite was Ma. I loved her. She helped raise me. Throughout my life, she became my go-to because my dad didn't know anything about raising girls. Sorry, no one compared to her. Period. So, any woman really had to impress me. And maybe two came close. But this Sidechick was different. She knew she was a Sidechick. Yet, that wasn't the place she wanted. She wanted the Title. She wanted First place! He repeatedly told her he would Neva leave my ma. But she wasn't listening. Ma wasn't here, and she thought that was a door for her. She had a Plan, and because I was #Team Ma, I guess I messed up her plan.

See, everyone knows how close my dad and I are, he listens to me, and I have influence over him because we have trust. He's my Idol because he saved me and my sister's life when we were younger. So, all the women try to get along with me if they really like my dad. But isn't that how it's supposed to be anyway? Shouldn't a Potential wife want to get along with the daughter? They can both help each other to help him too. Right? Right. With Ma, that's how she was. She was always the same, the sweetest woman I knew.

But, as I said, she was different. On the first day, I met her over the phone. I decided to visit Dad from Atlanta, and my sister came down as well just because we hadn't seen each other for a while. And, we are all lying on ends of my dad's bed talking and catching up, and she called for the 20th time, no lie, and said BOBBY, come get me. He said, "Nah, I'm chilling, gonna spend time with my girls. She started yelling. COME GET ME, COME GET ME, COME GET ME!

My Dad refused, and she said, "What are you doing fucking your children?"

At, that moment, I knew something had happened to her as a child. For someone to think that my Father has or would ever touch me inappropriately clearly doesn't think like a sane person. Why would that come out of someone's mouth, of all things? I'm sure I'm not the only one but, I pride myself that my

2

father and Uncles have all behaved in an appropriate manner and would never violate me or my sister.

So, immediately, I stepped back. I said something ain't right. And, I asked Dad, how can you want to be with someone who accused you of sleeping with your kids?

He said it, "Don't mean nothing. She's crazy. And she has a hard time trusting men. She had had two nervous breakdowns and got really hurt. She is just acting out."

If you could see my side-eye at the moment. I had never seen my father accept bad behavior. He didn't accept any from me or my sister so why now? He kept making excuses for her demeaning and belittling him????? That was strike 1. Why?

I went on back to Atlanta and kinda distanced myself from my dad. I didn't like what I was seeing; I was seeing someone totally different. Something was off but, I couldn't put my finger on it. When I did visit, I could never see my dad alone. She always wanted to be around my dad and our home, and when he made those three calls a day to Ma in Atlanta, she would always be in the room while he talked to her.

She would always be sitting in a corner listening to his conversation with ma! Creepy, right? I walked in on her one day... I didn't even know she was upstairs at the time. He told

3

me he was on the phone with Ma. I walk into the room, and she is sitting on the corner of the bed, with her finger Over her lip, telling me to be quiet! She was just sitting on the bed listening to him.

I said, "What in the Hell?"

He told me to be quiet. I bit my tongue, trying to hold my mule. And then I quickly turned to her. My face said it all. She looked real creepy and desperate at the same time to me from that point forward. I wanted nothing to do with her; that was strike 2.

Chapter Two

THE HOUSE WAS NOT A HOME ANY LONGER

Today my dad wanted me to go out to eat with him and his new Sidechick. I was skeptical cause all I heard was her yelling at him and him yelling at her. And I didn't see any reason why my dad was ok with this toxic environment. See, my dad messed around with the Sidechick 30 years prior and left her alone then because she was crazy and tried to ruin things. She was married then, so it was just a cut buddy situation. He said he thought she might be different since she is on medication now and decided to give her another try. I looked at my dad like, why would you want to give someone like this who clearly has mental issues another chance? I shook my head the entire trip. Every time my dad got above 60 mph. She began screaming and oh lawd, Bobby, OH lawd, my nerves.

And, he would be yelling at her, "Will you shut up!" I'm sitting in the back seat of the Lincoln, feeling like I'm in the twilight zone.

I asked, "Are you ok?"

She says, "My nerves are just all torn up; that's why I can't drive."

I felt like there was absolutely no reason for this relationship to be going on. My Dad is a quiet, sweet man. He loves peace; we have always had a peaceful life. Yes, there were a lot of women in his life at all times during my childhood. But they helped take care of us while he was raising us. Everyone knew their place and played it accordingly. So why would he bring this demon into our lives with all of her mental issues? She didn't work; he always loved an independent woman.

She lived in the projects and received a monthly mental health check, yet he lived in a Big house with five bedrooms. He liked a quiet woman who was feisty and not afraid of getting in his shit. She was a nervous wreck, so why? And she yelled at him repeatedly over the phone multiple times a day. It was okay to call. But she called just to make sure he was in place because she didn't trust him.

I'm sitting there talking to my dad about business, and this woman calls and says, and I kid you not, "Where you at Bobby? What are you doing, Bobby? Who are you talking to, Bobby?"

All in one sentence.

My Dad answered her questions most times. Like clockwork, until he got tired, and then he would start yelling at her to stop this foolishness every day. I would just sit back, watch, and listen because I was so confused. I tried to be fair in accepting her, but I couldn't find the positives. There were none, and you got to understand I'm on that left ear talking. #Team Ma all the way. I was always comparing her to Ma. I tried to look past all the craziness once again, but something ain't right with this woman. I still did not understand the need for this drama. There ain't no benefit to it. At all! Just stress.

I constantly moved from home to Atlanta between 2013 and now. I'm ambitious, and Atlanta is the place to be for an entrepreneur. And, you got to work to be who you want to be. I hadn't found my purpose yet. Every time I moved home, it was good because I had a home I was raised in and could come to at any time. It was my home. But during 2013 and now, the house felt so different. I could feel a coldness that I couldn't explain. I started feeling physically sick, as if I was gonna pass out from this smell. It was a horrible musty musk smell and mothballs.

And, Dad said, "I like the smell?"

Whatever it was, it made me sick. So I couldn't stay in the house. If I came home, I stayed with my mommy. This went on for months because every time I visited, I got physically sick. It was on the walls and curtains.

One day, it happened. I remember coming home yet staying with my mom because I felt something. I went to see my dad. I had no keys, really didn't even think about it. Cause Dad was always home. I went to see him, and he didn't answer the door. He called me about 2 hours later and said, "Yea, what's up?"

I said, "I came to see you."

He hesitated and then said, "I know, I didn't want no company?"

Faints quickly, wake up!

"How, didn't you want no company in our home? Dad, what is going on with you? You would never say, I couldn't come home?"

I'm thinking hard now. I never believed or practiced any roots of Witchcraft before. I felt it was an insult to make someone do what you want by controlling them. I heard stories, saw this guy walk in my hometown for about 20 years, all because of

roots. But didn't practice it. I felt God was good, and no matter

the problem, he will fix it. But when my dad told me that I

couldn't come home. Knew at that moment. I needed the help of

the unknown. Roots and Witchcraft. I began searching.

Chapter Three

2016, THE LIE

"During my travels and moving back home when things got rough or moving home was easier or I was just not settled in my spirit yet. My soul was restless, and I could not find peace. I sought it but, no matter what, I didn't find it. No home was my home. I literally would come home and get so involved in my family and, it became so stressful because I always had to say, "What about me?"

And, I got tired and angry and frustrated with all of the responsibilities of home, I would flee. I'm gone again, Atlanta called me again, and I would leave...But, don't get me wrong, I love the dynamic of my dysfunctional family. They keep me busy and motivated. But, sometimes, it can be too much. I selfishly chose myself about four times because the same thing would occur over and over again. I truly wanted to be home...But, it was too much work for one person.

No one could see that, no matter what I said. Especially my Dad. I became the billpayer, way maker, regulator, secretary, situation fixer, and everything, and he had a woman? Why do I always have to work so hard if you have someone you sleep with and be around every day? That is her responsibility, not mine. My Dad said she didn't know how to pay bills or handle business. She's only worried about who I'm sleeping with, not all that.

So, I asked, "Well. Why are you with her? If the only thing she can do is cook and fuck? If she can't help you, why are you wasting your time? There are plenty of smart women out there. You should not have run away from Ma for this woman."

He said, "I don't know! For the life of me, I don't know why I'm with this woman."

I thought about all of this that day, and it wore on me. I grew tired of being the only one working, so it seems. If it wasn't for my Daughter helping, I would have been lost. As I said, normally, I would leave because of the responsibilities, but this time it was something else. I knew my dad needed me there.

In 2016, something happened. My life changed forever. At first, I thought it might be due to menopause. In 2012, I had to have a full hysterectomy due to endometriosis and fibroids. It put me into full menopause but, I didn't really notice a change in me. I could wear white again and not be afraid of messing up my pants. The fibroids were a lot of pain and, in the end, a period nightmare.

After I had had enough, I decided it was time to get rid of the pain. I was healthy and happy and could have sex every day if I wanted to. I'm good. I thought. But, I still felt very different inside... Bad Things started to happen to me. I lost so much, and simple things were going wrong, which made absolutely no sense. Nothing made sense. When the hard times came, and I needed to move back home. I could go home. A lot of people can't but, I could. So that's just what I did... I was single, trying to make it but lost my job, so why struggle when I had a place called home? I called my dad.

The purpose of my dad building our family home was to give refuge to his kids. He always wanted them to have a home. That was his goal when he was gambling. And he built this house with all of his winnings for his kids. He has four kids hence four bedrooms to allow each kid a place to stay If they lose a job or fall on hard times. My dad wanted all of his kids to have a place called home. I called my dad up and told him I needed to come home because I had lost my job.

12

My Dad said, "Is there some other place you can stay?"

I said, "No, I wanna come home."

He said, "Jen, I can't do it!"

To say I went off is an understatement. But I know it went something like this:

"What do you mean you can't do it? Dad, why can't I come home?"

"Because "Samename" is here, and I don't want any problems."

I sighed. "Samename"

When he called her name, I thought he referred to Ma cause they share the same name. But, Ma would never turn me away. When he told me the last name, my tongue fell down my throat. I noticed I didn't hear from my dad much. I was distancing, but normally he would reach out a lot because I'm his Ace. Righthand man, I owe him my life, and he taught me how to do everything. He taught me how to hustle, and I'm forever grateful. So we were very close. But, when this woman came along, it changed.

In 2016, I barely got a call, only on April 26th cause he forgot my birthday was on April 25th. When I called him to come home, I expected him to say sure, come home, see you soon. Not,

13

"I can't do it." You raised me, Sir; you told me I could come home anytime. I'm lost. But I let it go and got off the phone with him.

On that particular day, I was getting off work. I walked out of Xfinity and headed to my car. As I walked, a woman approached me.

She said, "Excuse me, do you read your bible?"

I said, "No, not really."

She said, "You should." She gave me her business card and said, "Come see me. You need help!"

I said, "Ok," but brushed it off; something told me to keep the card.

I went to Thomson the next day to talk to my dad in person. Cause I really needed to understand his decision. If I had done something to him, I wanted to know, so I could apologize and discuss, but there was nothing. I knocked on the door, and he answered, and as we walked up the stairs, he told me Sidechick was there. The routine was he got off work, picked her up, and she stayed until he went to work, and that cycle repeated.

I walked into the room, and she was under the sheets naked. And, the room wreaked of the awful, musty musk smell throughout the house. It was her, she had it on her, which when he touches her, it's on him. Once again, I felt sick. My head began to hurt... I don't know if it was from that musty musk smell or what but, I became dizzy. I asked my dad to speak with him downstairs.

He said, "Guess what? You got another sister."

My immediate response was from who? For a period of time, it seemed like I got a sibling every year. So I wasn't shocked.

He said Sidechick says, "Her baby girl is my daughter. I looked over at Sidechick and smiled and said, "Oh yeah, When? I wanna meet her, and she needs to know she's my sister."

She refused. I said, "Why not?"

"Because she doesn't want her husband to know because he will ask for all of his child support back!"

I said, "Dad, I need to see you downstairs."

We went downstairs, and he tried to convince me that Francheska looked like us. I told Dad we needed to get a DNA test first. I'm gonna go and meet her and talk to her. Why is everyone asking how that is my business? Because I was the one that was hand bread to be Executor of my Father's estate. I was the responsible one that my Dad trusted, and if I was gonna be in charge of his estate, I needed to know who my siblings were.

I knew my dad was indeed a rolling stone and a gambler, so it came with the territory. I knew multiple children would come forward because he has worked all his life and built a fortune. Who wouldn't want a free ride? And. I was alright with that, Cause I would handle it. But I wanted to know. Let's get back to the conversation. I asked my dad why he would believe a cocomamy excuse like that? You know that man ain't gonna Ask for no money back, she lies.

He said, "He will, 'cause they were still married."

I said, "She is only telling you this to gain your love and trap you."

"Why now, after 30 something years? And, why not tell her who her father is? You spending time with her and her family, ain't you? I know you are."

He said, "Yes!"

I said, "This woman is up to something, and I'm going to find out what that is."

Finally, I said, "Now you have a purpose for staying with her. Dad, I don't trust her. We need a DNA test."

He said, "Look, Jen, let me handle it!"

I said, "Ok, while looking at my Dad and wondering who he was?" Cause my dad would never claim a kid if DNA was not done.

Chapter Four

THE REVEAL

When my Dad first got my sister and me, we struggled. My dad is known in our hometown for being a card game legend. When my Dad first got us, he was lost on what to do with an 11-year-old and a 13-year-old girl. He was out in the streets, and even when he was married to my mommy, he was never home.

He came home definitely on Christmas Eve to get our presents ready and dance on Christmas morning with my mom. I remember hearing "Merry Christmas Baby" and laughing and jumping with my sister while they danced. Because that's how we knew it was Christmas. Christmas morning was always the best morning of my year. But, gambling and women took my father away from us many nights. I only had my mom. I was devastated when she gave us to my Dad.

But, it turned out to be the best thing she could have ever done for us. My Dad didn't even know what to do when my sister got her period. Neither did I. We weren't taught much about feminine things 'cause we were still pretty young. And that's where Ma came in. She taught us how to be Young Ladies, told us all about feminine things. She didn't have to do as much work with me because I was a Diva from birth with a high I.Q. I was far more aware due to the molestation that I faced as a child. I knew a lot of things no child my age should have known... But, even at a young age, I knew how to turn lemons into lemonade and learned to benefit myself.

But, my sister was a challenge because she had a mental defect. As a child, I was always spoiled. I remember not going to kindergarten the entire year because I got a headache on the first day, and my dad made my mom come and pick me up from school, never to return. My Dad told my mom not to whip me and not send me back to school. Those kids gave her a headache, and she doesn't need headaches.

My mom was mad as hell. I was a Daddy's girl. I skipped Kindergarten and went straight to first grade. They dressed me in pretty dresses and cute ponytails. My sister would be dressed the same but, no one noticed her. I was always the star. For this reason, my sister resented me. And, my mom tolerated more picking than I did to my sister. So I always felt I was right. When

I went to live with my dad, I became responsible for my sister because although I was younger, I was the older sister mentally, and she became sort of my child.

At first, when he got custody of us, we would stay with one of his Girlfriends for weeks at a time. He then got married to Sarah. Sarah had two kids. We stayed for my 8th-grade year. I had to change schools in order to go to Warren County High. I hated it because I didn't want to move, and my sister and I were definitely the stepchildren. They filed for divorce because her kids were unhappy, and we were homeless once again.

We stayed with my Aunt and Uncle for the summer, and then we moved to Norwood with another Woman in 1986. She was named Connie. She was the sweetest woman I know. I had had my daughter Charantiga by then and she helped me take care of my Baby Girl. She loved us all and showed it. I knew about Ma but couldn't tell Connie under the Family Code. I was sworn to secrecy, kinda like an NDA of dads. When they became friends, I said, well, I guess Dad got it all figured out? (Throws up hands.) And left it alone but always gave him the side-eye when he talked about his women knowing about each other.

Connie and I argued one day. I still can't remember why. Either way, I'm sorry about it. But, it got so bad, we had to move that day because it turned physical. I was 16, grown, wild, having fun, and working with a Baby. You couldn't tell me anything, So, I hardly listened. I remember repeating 12th grade because I fought a girl the last two weeks of school and got suspended. I just felt pretty face, tight in the waist. Let's get this money. Crazy, but I wasn't having as much sex as I was accused of tho.

The hustle and getting money without having to sleep for it was the game with me. I was pretty trouble, and my dad knew that because he trained me to be such. I was trained on both sides, how to be a Diva and how to be a Hustler and Player. And do all 3. My Dad always stood by his kids. No matter what happened, he chose his kids.

When Sarah asked us to leave because her kids were unhappy...

He said, "Girls, pack your things with no hesitation. When Connie said, "All of you have to go."

He said, "Pack your things."

And, we did...We went back to my Aunt's for a while, and then dad found us a house next to National Guard Armory.

I was far more advanced than 16. All because I was raised by my Dad. He advanced me in a sort of kinda Hustler Boot camp, and all I had to do was listen. He taught me what the game was and how to counter it. What to let him know and always had my back. The only thing I hated that he tried to teach me was cards. I failed horribly because It wasn't a book... He told me, "It's ok, your brain will make you a whole lot of money one day!"

I feel like I ended up really being the boy he never had. I was taught how to survive and get money. I ran the house while he was gone. I remember meeting Sidechick for the first time. Yes. I met this skank before when I was a teenager. I walked out the door after dad came home from gambling one night, and she was in the car. She was young, which made me question my dad. The women are usually much older.

He said, "She was about six years older than you."

I normally didn't meet anyone unless he was serious about them. But, since I came outside, I guess I caught them. She was married, so they were creeping, but that came with the gambling lifestyle. That is all I knew. But, what's crazy is he was yelling at her then also. I remember that's what stood out about her to me. He was yelling at her to stop asking me so many questions. He called her all kinds of crazy. He slammed the door and told her he was taking her to the car, and they were gone.

I became my Father's protector, so to speak, in his eyes. I held the secrets, the money, and "act right if need be."

In 1995, I got married to a soldier and moved away to NC. Although I lived in Augusta before I got married, Dad and I were still close. I was still his right-hand man. If we both needed anything, we were there for each other. He saved our lives; therefore, we owed him our lives, and loyalty was the only option.

When I moved to NC, I missed my Dad one day, And, thought of him so much. I looked up, and he was pulling up in my driveway. I was so shocked; he said, "I wanted to surprise you and do it all by myself."

Ma called me that night to tell me how hard of a trip he had but was determined to see us. But, he missed us so. I was overwhelmed with love on that day. A few weeks passed, and I received a call about 10 pm from Dad. He was hysterical and cussing up a storm. He told me a woman had put a shotgun to his head and stole his car. She got a key made to steal the car. She called Ma's husband and told him about my dad and Ma. And, told Ma that she would buy him one if she wanted him to have a car.

He said, "I need you to come to get my car back."

I agreed with no hesitation. I went into a rage cause daddy knew he had no business messing with this woman. Everybody knew she was crazy. The proximity of her location should have told him she was definitely not someone he needed to be fooling with. But, once again, that fast lifestyle. He didn't care. He just wanted all the women that were paying. And that was the only requirement. You pay, and you help take care of his kids. He was a gambler; he needed money at all times. And, he ain't wanna hear no excuses.

I hopped in my car and made the 4-hour drive. After locating the car at her friend's house, I got the car and took it back to my dad's house and waited for her to come. I parked my car on the opposite side of the house. She never knew I had come home to get her altogether. When she came over here and knocked on the door...I could hear her saying, "What I told him. Who told him to put this car back in his yard?"

I opened the door and said, "I did!" I cursed her out so bad and dared her to come forward. We called the police and waited as her husband watched in silence.

I said, "Nate, you know this ain't right."

He said, "I have nothing to do with it, Jennifer."

Oh my God. I finished with the police officer and told her she never stepped foot on my dad's property again and meant every word of it. See, I was my dad's equalizer. He was the biggest Hustler who took so many risks that kept us in the dark many times, kept him walking to work from running out of gas, and kept fast food on our table from the ladies 'cause he was always broke. But, when it came to handling crazy women, he was weak as a lamb. He was a sweet man. But, when he snaps, everyone should run. When it came to women, though, he always called his baby girl. He needed muscle. And, in my family, I am that person. Yes, lil ole me. Why? Cause my mouthpiece was deadly and will make a motherfucker think twice.

The one he calls when he needs a situation handled. And, although I felt he was just as crazy for messing with those crazy women. I had his back. And, no woman was gonna hurt my dad. Problem solved.

When my Dad told me to just leave it alone about the DNA test, of course, I ignored him. I left his house and went straight to HP Pelzer, where he told me Franchesca worked. She hadn't come in yet. I waited for 2 hours, and finally, they told me she called out of work that day.

I called Dad and asked where did she live on Salem Road. He told me I went there, and my knocks were unanswered. I sent Facebook messages, and no response. I wanted to meet her. There are three more potential children of my Father's who do not know they are his children, and they all have the same traits and mannerisms. I felt if I met her, I could tell. I called Sidechick, and she said she would tell her. After a while, I just gave up. If she really was my sister, why didn't they want to know for sure? So until the DNA test is done, she is no sister of mine.

Chapter Five

THE BREAKIN

The reason I am who I am is because of how I was raised, concerning my dad and his Ex. Sidechick, Some said I was this way because I wanted to control my Dad. I wanted to control who he sees and his life. But. As I write this book, I assure you all I wanted was for my dad to be treated right and loved correctly. Who doesn't wanna see their parents happy? I didn't care who he dated. If Ma knew and accepted it, that's their business but, they are gonna treat him right. He is older and much slower and deserves peace in his life and home. He needs a life partner now. He will always love Ma. But, he dates other women. I'm happy to welcome someone strong and loving who will care for my dad. And take the load off of me. Come on. I love him. And I do a lot for my dad, and he does too. Love him, not cause drama. He just wants peace, and he can't get it with her. But, once again, why is he accepting it?

Because I'm biased knowing what he has done for me, why would I wanna stand by and see my father consistently verbally abused? That is Elder abuse. If we really wanna get technical about it. He was constantly being accused of cheating. And, Humiliated in front of his neighbors and family. She was yelling at him all the time on the phone and in person. It's debilitating, to say the least,

BUT, what I couldn't accept is WHY he accepted it.

All my life, I was taught differently. My father taught me a lot about everything. Relationships and what not to tolerate ever, how to move on. Quickly. I admit I'm the total opposite. But, he had some good points. I wasn't trying to control him. I love him infinity, and he always will be protected if I see something ain't right. So, that's a moot point. I would do the same for my entire family. Treat them right. They are good precious people to me. I stand on that!

Reflection: Let's go back further to help you understand what this woman did to us.

At the end of 2016, I received a call from my dad telling me. Sidechick carved her initials in the dresser desk and stabbed his chair.

I went off; he says "Don't worry, I'm done with her." But then I saw the furniture when I came home a few days later. What sane person carves their initials in someone's furniture? Or Stab the inside of a chair, so you are surprised. Ha Ha! Nope. I wondered if she bought this stuff at first and then asked Dad, and he said no.

So, why in the hell did She do it?

He says, "She accused him of messing with A prosecutor."

Damn fool even called her and left two threatening messages, not even caring it was the law. And, she Is just his friend. Says he found it when he got home. When she came, they argued, and he made her leave.

She just wanted control. That is what this whole thing is about, Control. But, my point was the Crenshaw house could never be sold. Furniture will come and go. But why do I have to give away furniture with a psycho woman's name on it? This is unacceptable. She is no longer welcome in our home. And, rightfully so. We don't do cheap shit. We pay our way over here. We are not getting a mental health check cause we can't work. We work, we strive, we build.

Always took pride in myself that I had working parents. Who taught the value of working hard for what you want.

No one has time to have their house vandalized when they are angry. And, still, you allow them back in to do it again. But, still, my dad said, "Let me handle it. I need time to get out of this mess."

I said, "Dad. I don't see you getting out of nothing; we are at three years now. Something has gotta give."

Then Boom. His phone rings, and it is ma. She called Ma to tell her about their relationship. This woman is trifling as hell. Ma told her she had already heard about it. She said she be going to Dr's visit with him and my aunt and my uncle Bo (rip, I love u). She said he took her to Red Lobster for her Birthday. (Sn: I swear y'all, this ghetto shit is so beneath mean. I feel so insulted I gotta tell the story. Because this is totally different from my lifestyle)

She told her he stays with her every night. Ma said, "Good for you!"

"I know everything he says to you. And he's mine, and you're stupid."

Ma says, "Good for you, and if he is your man, then keep him from calling me." And, she laughed, click.

When I heard about this, that was the final straw. This skank had to go. Not only are you doing things to hurt my dad, you calling people, informing and threatening people for whatever reason you chose. And you called my Ma! But, dad said again, "Let me handle it; I need time to get out of this mess."

"How much time do you need? She is doing all this crazy stuff and is crazy, and we need our home to be peaceful again. And, by the way, what is that smell? It makes me sick every time, it stinks, and it's all over you."

My dad said, "What smell?"

That's when I realized that something was up. Something ain't right.

"Why mothballs?" I asked.

He said, "She said she had seen some rats."

Lololok. I've never seen a rat in the more than 30 years I've been in this house.

"Unuh, no rats. It stinks in here. Smells like an old house with a stench." I laughed so hard as I started removing the mothballs. I had to take breaks 'cause I couldn't stay in the house for about 30 minutes at a time, or I would get sick when I was there.

I went back to Atlanta and continued working and living. I had my sister's son Lagearld now, so I was trying to get him taken care of him…But, I called my dad, and she made a noise and when I asked, "What was that?"

My father said, "She was there, what?"

Chapter Six

2017 – MY BED

One day I was cleaning my room. I know I had put the card in the drawer from Michelle, but somehow it ended up on my dresser, and I called Michelle. The one outside of Xfinity asked me to come to her office. I told her I could come Friday. She said, ok, hurry.

I said, "Well, if it's that urgent, I'm off today. I can come right now."

I arrived at her office; it was in a business shopping center, so I felt secure. She invited me back to her office, and I sat in front of her. She said I know you don't believe me, but there is a black cloud over you. I was like, "Huh."

She said, "Do you believe in roots."

I said, "I've heard of them but never practiced it."

She said there are two women; one is of English decent and one of Jamaican descent, and they are working roots on you. Blank face. I'm floored. I knew it was something.

She says, "I can't see their faces, but they are close to you. At least one is around you quite frequently. Be aware of your surroundings. I can see there is a woman that changes the color of her hair quite often."

Sidechick is notorious for this... looking like a clown most times...changing her hair color... After her weak performance every time I see her, of trying to keep up with the Jones' and broke... I remember when she told my dad we could go to family dollar and get some peel-on wood for his floor because he wanted hardwood.

I said, "I'm sorry, we don't buy cheap shit." I laughed at that clown.

Finally, I said, "Who asked her." Then, I asked my dad What's wrong with her? Cause he would never. She accused my dad of sleeping with me. So, I had no kind words for her. This woman is no match at all for him, so what was going on? Why were they still together?

I'm hearing things now from people about Sidechick. My dad's women were small petite, and feisty. They all worked and

34

had their own. But, they were all beautiful of Indian or white descent. He never had a woman that lived in the projects, didn't work, was fat, was accusing him every day, left and right, was loud or abusive or loud in appearance. And cutting up his shit! But, Sidechick would change her hair color to match her mood, I guess... It just never matched.

Her motives were clear. She wanted me gone. She would be mad at my Dad because he allowed me to come home. My dad behaved in a manner I had never seen. It was like he was a shell and only went to work. Chilled out. And went to her house and stayed in the Projects. Cause she couldn't come here. Since she damaged property, she wasn't welcome. Period. And as long as I lived there, he would have to go over there. And I wasn't playing about that!

Do not start, let me explain, when I was younger, I lived in the projects. I am not above it and never was. It served a need in my life at the right time. But I didn't stay there. I evolved and moved and got better. For me, the problem is I was insulting my father. He told me he never raised me to live in the projects. So why in the hell is ok with living in the projects. I was raised to never live in the projects. You can do so much better. Well, Buddy, you have a 5 Bedroom and two baths. But, you chose to live in the very place you forbade me all my life? He started arguing with me cause I was questioning everything. And he sounded just as dumb as her. He even accused me of stealing from him. I told him I felt guilty for taking a quarter from him. Where was this coming from? He told me I was just trying to control his life and he wasn't gonna stop seeing her; his life was good! Ok, you call Ma three times a day in front of Sidechick.

He said she understood. But she understands what I ask. She understands that Ma is the main and I love her, and she is sick? Dad, why did you leave Ma again? She got real sick, and she was staying here, and I couldn't be there for her. Little did he know I had talked to Ma. She told me my dad told her he didn't have time to take care of her. He had other things to do. This woman was with my dad for over 40 years. She moved out of her house to care for my nephew Lagearld when my Dad had custody of him. She earned the right for him to take care of her. He told her he was seeing Sidechick, and she had already heard everything. In fact, her family sees everything too.

She said she didn't know him anymore… the person he was becoming. He spends every day apologizing and checking on her, and get this, most of the time, she is listening. My dad was so messed up He quit gambling when she left. As long as Ma competed with the card game... He went full force into seeing Sidechick, but after Ma left... he showed Ma love three times a day. And all respect too. He hid Sidechick. Everyone thought he was still with Ma. Because he never took Sidechick to family events or out in public. Lol, it was to his house back to hers and go to doctor appointments and to eat in AUGUSTA but not Thomson.

If you can, Imagine going to different family events with My Dad, and he is always wearing the clothes Ma bought him and talking about her to everyone like he loves her so much and sleeping with Sidechick at night. He was a nervous wreck and so confused. He was a Mess. But, was 75% loyal to Sidechick, even if it meant going against me.

I heard that this woman would hang out at the Bootleggers on the backstreet of the projects. Bootleggers are a Jamaican couple. A woman and a man who sells food, beer, liquor, and practice witchcraft... She goes there and drinks all day! Hold up! Drinks all day? RED FLAG NUMBER 99! MY Dad doesn't even like women that drink. Period. Don't know what happened, but any woman in his life never drank, never smoked, and didn't do drugs...So dad......how are you getting by all the kissing? This was all too much. I also heard this woman travels back and forth from Jamaica. Bingo. Then I was told she stabbed her previous boyfriend.

I asked Dad about that as well, and he said, "She said he beat her."

Everything I said, my Dad countered or defended this woman. She started going to my Uncles and Aunts and Dad's doctor visits with my dad and eventually started caring. For my uncle Bo, I found this strange also. How is she certified? What nursing work has she done? What man wants his brother's woman wiping his brother's ass or seeing his penis? It was all weird.

Dad said, "That because his sister shouldn't see all that, she had to bathe him!"

My dad started taking her to bathe him and cook for him as he got sicker. But get home and tell my Dad his other brother ought to be ashamed. She was only doing it for show. Or she wouldn't complain. But, she took pride in integrating into my family. She built relationships. It took time, but it was happening.

She wanted complete control of my dad. So whatever she had to do. And, I was in the way. She would even go as far as sacrificing her own because come on now. I've learned a lot while going through this hell. When you wanna put roots on someone, you wanna control them. Therefore, in order to get what you want, you must sacrifice one of her own.

I often wondered why her husband got sick so suddenly when she got with my dad in 2013. What's even stranger is why is she taking care of him? They hate each other, right? Questions were building up, and why shouldn't he know about his kid that may not be his own. My dad always spoke badly of him. As if he was competition. Why? I guess cause she was still taking care of him. But, once again, why did he accept it?

She said, "What's up with your back?

Reflection: A bump came up almost in the middle of my back, and my daughter tried to bust it for me since I couldn't reach it. One day she got something out of it, and it was wood. I don't know how but it was a piece of wood. And, no doctor could understand that.

When she said, "What's up with your back?" I showed her the bump, and she said, "That's how they entered you."

I got scared. She said, "Do you see things out the corner of your eye sometimes?"

I said, "Yes."

She said, "Someone who is your friend has passed. His name is doubled."

"Buck Buck?"

"Yes!"

I cried as I wrote this. I loved Buck Buck, but, I'm saving him for the autobiography. She said he is around you at all times, fighting for you. He is like a soccer goalie around you. Just hitting it away. He says don't be afraid. He is protecting you. But, we must get rid of what was in our back because it will continue to grow. Y'all, when I tell you, I was scared and comforted at the same time. Because I knew who the two women were, and the only way I could have gotten something on my back was when she hugged me once or My Bed.

When I moved back home in 2016, I experienced yet another process of I'm moving back home. But, I was coming from NC. My daughter needed me to move with her and the kids, and I left NC and came home.. something kept bringing me HOME. And, I didn't know then, but I'm glad I know now. God kept sending me home for a reason.. it all makes sense... These evil women have a spell on me and my father. One to get rid of me and make him love her. It further explains why everything I do fails, why I don't feel like myself anymore..why fashion runs a gamut with me when I am the jazziest B around for my age. Everything on the left side of my body changed. It felt as I had a stroke. My memory was limited.

Then, I began falling for no apparent reason at all. I remember I tried to stand on the ladder and slid... I'm blessed because every time I fell... I always landed to in a way that would hurt me... but it was minimal damage at times. What was going on? I was in good health, and there was absolutely nothing wrong with me. I was still getting it. Yet, I was different. I saw the shadows in my right corner and left corner of my eyes and said, "Thanks, Buck Buck ♥"

I thought I was losing my mind. And, yet, I was steady fighting. I said my dad needs me if this really is true. She has them on his tail as well.. it explained why he shut his family completely out and doesn't wanna deal with us. Yet, he is spending all of his time with his supposed-to-be daughter and her family. I was like, what about us. But, after I told him I had a blowout, and he wouldn't come to get me. I felt like My dad had lost his mind... I knew he had changed. He wanted nothing really to do with us. He only wanted the Sidechick and her family...

I was sick, yet no doctor could diagnose me with stroke or anything related to my symptoms. I became less involved because I couldn't function. My mind didn't work the same way before. I was the alpha Female, yet somehow I got dumbed down. I was dating Racon at the time. He had moved back from Cali, and we reconnected. That was an absolute disaster, and honestly, he could have just been honest after that train wreck. I decided to go back and see Michelle. It was too much. I had two car accidents back to back where my driving record was spotless. I didn't believe it before, but it explained everything I was going through. I was going back and forth home. Buck Buck Died, and, Money became a problem, and I didn't know how to cope... I never sold a bag Worth 1000 for 500 so fast. I kid you not, but I had to survive; I'm a Hustler. I did it legally to survive. I made it work, and if I couldn't, I'm spoiled. I go back home and recuperate.

You see, you didn't have to pay bills at my Dad's house. You pay your bills because he says his are gonna get paid anyway. He wanted you to get on your feet. That's the dad I know. But I abused that privilege once, and he got me together quickly to the point of putting me out... It took me until 2013 to understand what that meant. "Just because you have a guaranteed roof over your head doesn't mean you take advantage of it." And. I started paying something while working back at the Authorized Verizon dealer and worked.. later transferring back to Atlanta. I worked there from 2013 to 2015.

The lady said, "They entered me through my back" That stuck with me all the way home. I kept trying to look in the mirror to see. But I couldn't. I then made an appointment with the doctor to try and remove it. When they did remove it, it had rapped almost around my rib. Stretched it out, and it resembled a snake. I was shaken. I now have a sunken scar. I don't have visible scars. Men will tell you my body is as smooth as a baby's bottom because I'm covered in cocoa butter at all times. So this scar baffles me because I don't have keloid skin. Normally a line at best. And I even had stitches. But I have a sunken scar. It's like a keloid reversed. Weird. Nothing makes sense to me at this point.

In 2015 I continued to work for the Retail Agent for a couple of years. I always had problems on my job with my coworkers and could not focus on the sales game enough to understand and made a lot of mistakes but, I tried and still was uneasy because of how I looked to people and the mistakes I was making that caused me a lot of money. There were plenty of times when I sold like a champion and became the District's number one sales manager, but then things became hard for me repeatedly. My sales were returned, and I ended up owing the company instead of making money. My finance dropped dramatically from chargebacks, and I wasn't making anywhere near the money I normally make due to chargebacks. I was suffering at work and at home too emotionally with no male companion, and whether that seems important or not, it was not normal.

Even my male friends, who were just friends, stayed away from me at all times. No calls, never showing up, my phone never rang no matter who I met, and whenever a conversation started, or we would plan to start a conversation, it always fell through. No man would approach me, call me or deal with me where there used to be a list. Something had to change, and the way I was losing money, I knew it wouldn't be long before the walls were going to come tumbling down. So, when my daughter called and said Ma, I wanna go back to NC, I knew that was the way to go. I put in my two weeks' notice as I did with any job. But this was different. I wanted to see if changing my location would make this thing go away. I was still falling for no reason. I was still mentally foggy and needed help, and maybe in my supporting her, she would support me and help me get over this funk.

We then moved to NC and got a 3-bedroom apartment in the Raleigh area, and things seemed to turn around, and then one morning, we woke up to my grandson saying, ma, what is wrong with my back? I looked at his back, and he had these big bumps and on his face was another bump. We began looking for the source but did not find it, and we thought it was odd but treated the bumps with alcohol and sent him to school. The following morning my youngest granddaughter was bitten under her left eye.

I said, "We may have bed bugs."

We began looking because we didn't do roaches and had never experienced bedbugs but, nothing else made sense. The following morning yet another grandchild was bitten. I then went to the rental office, and they scheduled a treatment which meant we had to remove all our clothes and small things to the patio and stay out of the apartment for 6 to 8 hours. For a few months after this, there were no more bites. We started living again without the fear of bites. But then my grandson and my daughter started arguing a lot, he was only nine but kept fighting with my daughter, and she asked that his dad get involved. He was from NC, and we moved there to allow him to have a relationship with his son.

One day he came to visit, and he heard my grandson over the phone curse at his mom, and he punched him in the chest.

I said, "No, stop, you don't hit him in the chest." And we got into it. I was very skeptical about allowing him to go with his dad that day out of fear of him getting hurt.

On the other side of things, I was constantly arguing with my daughter about people she was bringing to the house. I was still uneasy about people and their intentions, which did not change just because we moved across states. We constantly argued about the men she was bringing around her kids to. My daughter wasn't a person who sleeps around, but she had many male friends, and I admit, I felt kind of jealous because no one came to see me, and it put me into a depression. But I never really went out, so I blamed myself for not meeting anyone.

Then a friend of mine told me about this guy she wanted to meet because we had a lot in common. I then met June. He was a really nice guy. At first, we began seeing each other and hit it off great, and she was right; we did have a lot in common. He came to our Empire parties and all and was a great source of inspiration for me, He was so supportive, and I just loved his laugh, and all of a sudden, once again, after a few weeks, he changed on me as well and wanted nothing to do with me.

At, this point there was madness. I was once again saying what I do. Yet, he said I don't know while hugging me and leaving. And I never saw him again, and I didn't even try to contact him because I knew and just let him go. There was no need to continue until whatever it was, was off of me. I was always so loving and giving, but at some point, reality set in, and I began to think about what was wrong with me?

In an effort to explain this phenomenon, I knew I had answered my questions. Whatever was happening to me was in me, and no matter what state I went to until it was out of me, nothing would change.

Then one day, my grandson came into the room and began getting bitten again. I went to the rental office yet again, they treated again, we removed our things, and after they treated the next day, he started getting bit again. I then thought something was going on here. Why do the bedbugs keep coming back? I visited all of my neighbors; it was a quad of 4 apartments, and all of them told me that bed bugs were a problem because they were in the wall, and every apartment had had at least four treatments. The reason being is that the bed bugs run from one treated apartment to the other, and this has been a problem for years. The Management company lied to me and acted as they had never heard of this before. I then went to the Managers office and said, "you knew. My kids were getting bitten up now for at least eight months, and you knew. I am going to sue you for this."

They scheduled yet another treatment with no explanation, only apologies, and I told them until my kids stop getting bitten, there will be no rent paid at all. This went on for at least six more months. We had a total of 8 treatments, and when my kids got bit the last time, I sued, and on the day of the court, they settled and wiped our nonpayment clean.

At that point, my daughter went her way, and I went mine, and I got a beautiful one-bedroom condo, and she got a 3-bedroom house with the money we received from the settlement. I was working at the North Carolina Department of Revenue, and as you already can imagine, I was constantly in a mess with people, and I am not an angel but, it always was made to seem as if I was causing the conflict. But most times, I was not, and I chalked it up to I can't win. No matter what I said, no one believed I was innocent. I argued with a lot of people at my work, too; I was always accused of one thing or another to the point my own daughter stayed away from me at work. I constantly asked her what she thought, and she would say, "Ma, I don't know what it is but every time you are around, something jumps off, and a problem starts but, I don't understand it because you don't deal with people but, everyone seems to have a problem with you."

I began to work two jobs to support my lifestyle and my new BMW, and I was happy. I now had two cars, a nice condo, two jobs, and I was as independent as I ever was and felt very successful. But I missed home. I didn't go anywhere, and my life was boring most time. I worked, slept, and was on repeat with no relationship for the entire time since June. I decided one day that NC was not for me anymore. It was still the same, and there was not an opportunity that I saw. Plus, I couldn't get along with anyone there. I was often misunderstood, accused, and lied on and most was so unexplainable I got tired of explaining, so what was the need for me to stay there? When I was alone by myself, I didn't have any problems, but there were always problems and misunderstandings anytime someone else was involved. I told my daughter I was going home, and she begged me not to go. I tried to continue, but I lost my job at the Department of Revenue two weeks later. They said they were making cuts, and I was one of them. I knew it was due to the incidents at work but, I couldn't fight it. I never got in trouble at work on any job for any reason. I was a professional but, this spell, this very twisted spell, was haunting me, following me, and creating havoc in my life once again. I called my dad and asked him whether I could move back home temporarily because things were not working out; I had lost my job and did not like NC anymore and wanted to come home.

He then said, "Let me think about it, Jen."

My first thought was, "Here we go again."

It was bad enough I had moved four times since 2013, but I had to beg my dad again to come home, and he was hesitating not because of him but because of the relationship he was in with Sidechick. He said, "Let me think about it because Sidechick doesn't want you here."

I told my dad Sidechick doesn't have a mule in this race; she doesn't own a thing and has no decision on what I do or if I can come home. And, what in the hell does she have to do with me coming home or not? Please explain.

He said, "She can hear you."

I said, "Do you want me to say it again? You have nothing to do with what goes on in our home; you are a visitor. You don't live there."

He asked me to give him a couple of days and then called and told me I could move back home. I began packing my things. Raycon came from Ga and moved me home. We argued all the way to Ga to the point he did even want to talk to me. He called me evil because I kept complaining about everything, even the way he drives. There was always a need to fuss and argue, and he was my intended target that day; and after we got to Georgia, when we got to my father's house, he parked the truck and got in his car and left.

I apologized because I couldn't understand why he was so mad with me.

He said, "What, you don't remember the things you were saying?"

I said, "What things?"

"It doesn't matter; I am gone."

We were forced to unload the truck by ourselves, and Raycon did not speak to me for a few days. When he finally called me, he asked what was wrong with me that day?

He said, "I came all the way to North Carolina to help you, and you acted like I was nothing to you."

I couldn't explain that either to him. I accepted the tongue lashing he gave me and apologized repeatedly; there was nothing I could do to defend myself. I was out of line on several instances, and I hurt his feelings. But it was as if I couldn't help it. My job was to annoy and destroy. And I did that with every person, no matter what they did or who they were.

Chapter Seven

MY BED
Continued...

When my dad let me come back home from NC, I knew it was gonna be a problem for me. I couldn't live in the house, but I was going to try. I had nowhere else to go. I always came with expensive things. This time a shiny BMW who I named Diva. She was a two-seater that I worked two jobs for. My Bedroom was fit for a Queen furniture-wise because it was solid oak and very sturdy. Finally beautiful, I work for it I pay for it. My mattresses were old, and Dad had bought some new ones for an old bed. So, I asked him whether I could use the mattresses. They both were King. He agreed, and I began to sleep on them with my Bedroom set.

On the first time sleeping on them, I was in my bed for five days. I was hurting in my lower back. The car accident had been two years back with no injuries. So why could I not get out of the bed? I felt drawn to the bed. I remember getting hit in the center of my head, Like a thump multiple times to let me know I wasn't alone. Someone was calling my name, always waking me up!

I had trouble walking cause the left side of my lower back hurt. My arm hurt, my chest hurt if I lay on my left side. I had constant pains. I was hurting and wondered why I couldn't move around and unpack my things. I thought I had injured something during the time I was moving, but Raycon moved most with my grandson. So no, but I was physically bound to this bed. So, there was no reason for me to be drawn to my bed. Finally, when I was able to get up. I remembered what Michelle said!

But, how am I able to stay in the house?

Michelle told me that to stay in the house. I needed to wash the walls with Pinesol. I didn't question it because she was so Truthful. But, I washed each wall in that house, especially my dad's room, where she had wiped the horrible musty musk smell on the curtains and the walls. You could even see the handprint still. And, I washed his curtains to kill the smell. I cleaned them, and she said, "Say, In Jesus' Name."

I don't practice it, but I felt the only way was to get rid of it was to fight it the same thing. Michelle was the first person who let me know what was going on. And I was ready to fight. I did everything she said. I was at peace because she wasn't allowed in our home. And I told her just that!

Raycon came and visited me from Atlanta. My Dad is old fashion and doesn't eva want another man to sleep in his house unless they are married. I respected it until I kept seeing Sidechick go up and down the stairs every day. And knowing what she did to me. The smirk on her face upset me but, I didn't care. I knew who and what the enemy was, and if I was gonna fight and win, I needed to be here around my dad. If she is this desperate, it's time to fight.

So, Raycon ended up spending the night. The next morning all hell broke loose. My Dad knocked on my section and said, "Rent money."

I said, "Dad, I'm sorry. We fell asleep."

He said, "I told you, and I meant it. I want him gone."

We argued.

I said, "What about the woman upstairs?"

He said, "You have nothing to do with that!"

I said, "I do. Why is she here and allowed to be here? I bet you can't answer that?"

And he paused, and she said, "I'll tell you why?"

I said I know what you did. She looked at me and said, "I sure did."

I told her, "From now on, you are only allowed on these stairs. Don't go in the kitchen or anywhere down here. You are not welcomed, and as soon as I tell my Dad, you will be gone."

The next two weeks were difficult. I didn't even feel comfortable in my own home. I was fighting my dad for the second time. And, it was all about a Sidechick. She's Evil, dad... She is trying to hurt me... I feel my dad knew he was hurting me in many ways by continuing to see the Sidechick. It was almost like she was fighting me through him. He was trying to stand up to me but couldn't understand because of unknowingly what was being done to him.

Things turned cold for us; I went to friends. I had to be told; he's not your Dad. If she's working roots on him, he is her. I worked two weeks and transferred back to Atlanta with my job. I couldn't do it. I got tired of the constant yelling coming from upstairs. My Dad yelled at her every time she called. She called every 15 minutes to ask his location, or it was always about another woman. He was lying to Ma every day. He doesn't see her. He doesn't spend the night with Sidechick in the projects.

You see, Ma was also calling him out on his disrespect. But, finally, in one of our conversations, she said she didn't know him; he was different and acted like he was losing his mind. Something was wrong, and she felt it.

This was when I told her about Michelle and my back. The fact I couldn't stay in the house because I would get sick. She then stated she doesn't believe in it, but be careful. I really didn't even have a chance to unpack, with work and a to-do list to complete. I had to restart my life all over yet again. God kept sending me home. And once again, I didn't know why? I put Dad's old bed back up before I left. I noticed that the mattresses looked fine, yet wherever I laid at there was a print of what looked like a greasy stain. My dad noticed it and said, "What happened to the mattresses?"

I said, "It happened while I was sick."

I don't know. I loaded my Uhaul back up and headed back to the A!

Little did I know that I would only be there a year and a half before I was sent home again.

When I went back, I worked for the Verizon Dealer for a short time and went to work for Xfinity. I was having a trying time with my Nephew Lagearld. I had rescued him from an abusive group home. He was being drugged to keep him from tearing up the place. He was my sister's child and someone who I loved but wasn't active in his life. I got him from the hospital and put him in the hospital, and detoxed him. He was a walking zombie. I loved him too much not to try and help him. He was dropped the day he was born and suffered Traumatic Brain Injury. Poor guy never had a chance. He had been in the system his entire life as mentally ill and, I found out he was in the top 5 of the most dangerous. He would have bad behavior and destroy everything in sight, and a lot of people often got hurt. But, when he told me, the guy beat him up. That's why he was falling and not the medicine. I questioned the group home, and they put him out that day.

As I said, I took him back and said, "Someone has to help this grown man, who is mentally five years old at best, to learn to be loved."

And no matter what anyone told me, I was determined to regulate his meds and show him he could have a great life. Someone just had to care. I just didn't know it would be so difficult. I first had to take him back because he needed 24-hour care; I had just begun Xfinity and was in training. I went and got him because he missed me, and I couldn't let these people hurt him. He had gone through so much. My dad even had custody for a few years, but he was too abusive. My main thing with my dad was you never spent time with him. You gambled; if it wasn't for Ma, he would be lost. She even moved in to help him, and he kicked her and broke her rib. And, she still stayed to help my dad out. He was a terror, so I understood why dad gave him back, especially after I had holes in the walls and broken vases that weren't cheap. But, God would send Angels by me to tell me for what you're doing, you're gonna be blessed. And, I started looking up. I got him the care he needed and medicines specifically to fit him, and we pressed forward.

Reflection: During this time, I also noticed that I constantly caught myself turning around in a circle. It was so strange, and no matter what I would do, I would walk forward, stop, turn backward because I forgot something, or even if I didn't, and I would turn back around. I always turned back to the left and came full circle. When I first started doing this, I attributed it to my mental state and how unbalanced mentally I was at this time;

the things I forged to get, I thought I was just moving too fast and forgetting things. But, this happened when there was nothing to get. Always walked forward, turned back left, looked back, turned completely back forward, and continued to walk on.

I constantly thought, whatever was done to me, this had something to do with it, but as always, I could not explain it and still live with it every day. My nephew finally saw it happening because I had never told him because I felt he wouldn't understand.

He said, "Nana, why do you turn around in circles so much?"

I let out a gasp of joy and said, "You see that, right?"

He said, "Yea, you just keep turning around in circles; it's funny but, why?"

It wasn't funny to me but, I can understand why he would say it. It looked absolutely crazy at times and for no reason, but this is yet another thing I endured. The significance of this to me was turning back to the left. Everything that has happened to me has happened on the left side of my body. There had to be a reason, and this had to be tied to what was going on with me. But then I thought, does the turning in circles have a meaning. Is it tied to all of the repetitive things that were happening, with the contractors, with me, with everything that I was going through? All bad things happened but, most of them happened the same way, the same situation, different people but yet the same things over and over again. Was the turning around every time and coming back full circle indication what was going on in my house with my dad?

This was just another part of my confirmation that this woman had something to do with it. "What did this spell have in store for me," I asked? And, I wasn't going to stop until I got the answer.

Chapter Eight

THE HEALTH SCARE

As I said, I had a very trying time with Lagearld and, once things calmed down, he started relaxing, and seeing that he was loved, things became easier. And, once again, the phone rang, and it was Dad. He said he had been having pain below, and the doctors thought it was his prostate. I got so scared. Anytime my Dad calls me, and his voice is heightened, he is scared. I had been going back and forth home now because of the new remodel.

Dad called me and told me he was ready to make his home look like what it should be.

He said, "I want It to look like I worked all of my life for this house. And, I went right to work."

"How are we gonna do this, Dad? You don't gamble anymore. Where is the money coming from?"

He said, "Let's call; I'm ready to use my 401k."

When I answered the phone, I was at work, and he began to tell me he had seen signs since 2013. But he ignored it.

He said, "The doctors need to do a test, and he wanted to wait because he hadn't met his deductible yet."

I said, "Dad, whatever it takes."

I was in tears cause I hadn't spoken to him after that big may lay at his house, where I told Sidechick she wasn't welcomed while I was there. So, I began at first to feel guilty. Then I said, dad let me know. A couple of weeks earlier, he called and had fallen. Once again, when he told me, I became hysterical. I went to my car, keys in the ignition, and was halfway out of my driveway, headed to see what was going on with my dad. He begged me not to come but wait to see what the doctor said about his eye. He fell off the porch and apparently knocked himself out, and damaged his eye. When he came to he called me to tell me what had happened. No one knew he was on the ground. Not even the witch upstairs, he says, but I was taking no chances. I called my daughter to go to the hospital to check on him. I was frantic and questioning everything because I was in Atlanta. And, It bothered me that I couldn't reach out and touch him if need be.

My daughter got frustrated at all my questions and said, "Well, if you wanna know so bad and are so concerned, come home."

I began thinking hard about my next move. When I got the prostate call scare, my mind was already half made up. But, I was 50-50 because I didn't wanna go through the trauma and drama of home. But, had finally gotten off my probationary period at work and was doing quite well; therefore, why would I want to leave my comfort zone.

I traveled between Atlanta and Thomson every other week due to the remodel beginning. I met a guy named Eduardo, who was my customer, and he told me he built houses. I spoke with him about my father's renovation, and he was ok with riding down behind me and seeing what I wanted to build. I had discussed with my Dad, and he agreed to let me handle the remodel because I knew what he wanted, and he felt confident it would get done right. When I first came down, I showed Eduardo the house and told him what I wanted to do. He took measurements and told me he would type up an estimate and send me the figures in the am. He left, and I went into the house to discuss with my dad what needed to be done. Immediately, I smelled the same smell I worked so hard to get rid of just a year ago. I became sick a lot quicker, so I told dad I needed to sit on the step instead of going inside the house.

Dad asked, "What's wrong?"

I said, "Dad, don't you smell that horrible musty musk smell?"

He refused.

I said, "Maybe because it's all over you, but I can't go in the house again, or I'll get sick."

He said, "Well, walk with me around back and come through the new part section. I need to show you something."

I retained my breath and followed him to the back part of the house I used to stay in. When I went in the door, he said, "Do you smell that?"

"OH MY GOD, what died?"

"I don't know. I was hoping you could tell me what it was?"

I said, "How?"

He said, "Because I can't seem to find it. I thought it was the rats she said she had seen. But, since you left a year ago, this is how it smelled."

I said, "Dad, this smell wasn't here when I left."

He said, "Well, a rat ain't smelled for over a year."

"Right." I searched, and the smell seemed to only be in my old room and closet. I opened the windows.

He said, "I've done that, yet the smell never goes away."

The old bed was nicely made with the mattresses I slept on. He had an old dresser in there, and the room seemed alright but, what was that dead smell? The front of the house reeked of the horrible musty musk, and the back of the house reeked of a dead rat or animal. This was too much for one day, and I told Dad I was leaving to go back home to Atlanta and would see him after I got the estimate from Eduardo.

Chapter Nine

UN-UH, NOT SO FAST!

I got back to Atlanta after a very trying day at my Dad's house. The smells were too much, and although one was explained away. The Sidechick was wearing the horrible smell, and because dad was around her, he was also wearing the same horrible smell. I know now that she had to have put it there in order for the smell to also be on the walls and curtains in my dad's room. The other smell was yet another mystery.

When I left my dad's house to move back to Atlanta, everything in my section smelled like perfume, yet we couldn't understand the dead animal smell that had reeked in the back part of the house.

Eduardo sent the estimate as planned on the following day, and I became very excited. The total amount was in the range of $30,000 to give my dad's home a total renovation along with the garage and gable porch. Dad and I talked, and he said all he had ever wanted was a double-car garage. In return, I always wanted a gable porch to allow me to relax and feel the breeze.

I said, "Of course, I won't charge you. But I want something out of the deal."

We reached an agreement, contacted Eduardo, and then discussed the payment options and a start date the following Monday.

My Dad wasn't a businessman to the degree where he understood how to pay for things of this magnitude. He only relied on paper bills to even know what bills needed to be paid every month. Since he wasn't savvy on banking and deposits, I had to make another trip to get the funds cheque-cashed, contracted, signed, and deposited into Eduardo's account.

We were all set and ready for the remodel to begin. We bought all materials and only paid for labor. My Dad felt this would be the cheapest way. I couldn't disagree with him because I had never done a remodel before, so I was clueless. But I wasn't clueless about people. Eduardo had shown me his website, had given me a business card, and had even signed a contract with both my Dad and me, but I couldn't be too sure because this was some of my dad's life savings, and I would never forgive myself if I was wrong.

I got a confirmation text from Eduardo that the deposit was paid and that he was ready to start. He said that he would be down the following day to see what was needed and order supplies. We agreed to pay for the tractor needed to finish the footing and the gravel to be replaced in the driveway and the materials. Eduardo was to build the garage and gable porch in two weeks. I was skeptical due to the possibility of rain, but my Dad being the trusting one, planned and scheduled to be there until the job was done.

Since I was back in Atlanta now, Sidechick could come and go as she pleased, and I asked Dad about it prior to agreeing to do the renovation because I wanted her nowhere in my sight or around me at any time. Yes, I know it's his house, but I needed to remain safe as long as I was at my Dad's.

I knew he didn't believe me because he didn't believe in roots just as I didn't, but nothing else could explain how he wasn't my Dad anymore. Nothing could explain how he would allow someone to violate us and give her a pass. Nothing could explain how when he had that horrible musty musk on him, he could argue with her from 1 pm, when he got off work, till 8 pm, because he got tired of the accusations and questions. But, around 10 pm, he could do nothing but wanted to stay in the projects, yet every night, nothing could explain the hole in my back and the snake-like cyst removed from my back, or the fact that I got physically sick if I stayed in the house for more than 30 minutes at a time.

Finally, nothing could explain why I was responsible for handling his business alone if she was constantly in his home. It just didn't add up and did not start until 2013 when dad made Ma leave.

I went back to see Michelle when I first moved back to get started, but her business was closed, and she was gone. I called the number on the card, and it was disconnected. I hadn't called or gone back to her because I had got the cyst removed and felt that since I was out of the house, I would be ok. I mean, I didn't know any better either way.

I felt I was ok until I came on the weekend before the renovation was to start. I got sick again the first night after sleeping in my dad's old bed with the same mattresses that I left when I moved back to the A. I stayed in bed this time for only one day but, once again, I had a hard time moving, especially the left side of my body. I left my dad's house the next day and moved my things and myself to my mommy's.

This wasn't over, and once again, I started searching again for someone to help me. *"Help us,"* I thought. Imagine trying to help yourself, and another loved one who felt there was nothing wrong. There was nothing wrong with him, of course, because he hadn't suffered as I had, but I couldn't give up. There was no way I could get rid of what was making me sick, to know who was doing it to me and allow them to keep control over my dad.

I began speaking to my best friend, Julia, about what was going on at my Dad's. I told her about the smells and the visits. I even told her about Michelle. She was highly against anything or anyone I had to pay for services to remove any spell. She would tell me about it being in the Bible and how God could remove these spells. At that time, my faith wasn't strong. When I was younger, I grew up in a holiness church but had gotten away from religion when I had a bad experience at my mommy's church. I didn't believe in preachers cause I trusted very few people. When she began talking to me, I wasn't listening most of the times.

I needed relief, and I needed it now. I even thought about putting something on Sidechick to make her go away. But, my conscience wouldn't allow me to follow through on it. I wasn't evil. I wasn't someone who would hurt people. I just wanted me and my dad to be healed and released from whatever this witch had done. I just wanted her gone for good.

"Help me, help me," that's all I kept saying to Julia.

She answered, "Read your bible. Witchcraft is clearly mentioned in the Bible."

After I told her about my Dad's disbelief, she said, "It's understandable, but there is no way anyone can believe in God and not believe in the devil.

She said, "You need to find someone in a church that can help you. And, be very careful, do not let your dad know what you are doing."

I thanked her and hung the phone up, and thought about it. I told my mommy what she said and explained how I didn't understand why my Dad wouldn't listen to me.

Mommy exclaimed, "Cause that's not your Dad!"

Chapter Ten

Conclusion of,

"UN-UH, NOT SO FAST"

My Mommy is a God-fearing woman. There are a few things about her I never question, such as if she speaks on your name or a word from God. When she told me repeatedly that she knew my father, I knew that she was telling me the truth. She spent at least 20 years with him, and they had some of the most unbelievable moments in the past. So, when she speaks of him now being different, it means God has told her the same. She also told me to seek God instead of someone that deals with Witchcraft. She had experienced people doing evil things in the past, and she knew what worked for her, i.e., God.

But I didn't have time to hear that. Maybe, I didn't want to hear it. I was losing faith every day. Something had to be done and quickly because I was losing my dad, day by day. I wanted him back. I decided I was going to do whatever it took to get him back to himself. And that was that.

When Eduardo said he ordered the materials and I asked for a receipt and didn't get it, I began to feel uneasy and questioned him. Where is the purchase order? Where are the materials that should have been delivered? When nothing was produced, I got a gut feeling that something was terribly wrong. The one thing I never wanted to do was fail my father. Also, this was a lot of money. I called Eduardo the next day because he was supposed to dig the footing for the garage, and he hadn't shown up yet. I called repeatedly but received no answer. We paid for an excavator from the local Tractor supply company, and Eduardo was supposed to pick it up when he got to Thomson.

I received another call later on from Dad saying he had busted one of his pipes the day before and had to turn the water off. I was like, *wow, what?*

He said, "While he was digging the footing, he dug too deep. I thought that was odd since Eduardo built houses.

Dad said, "he said that he will be back in the morning to fix my pipe."

I said, "Dad, I am sure he could have gone back to Ace Hardware and fixed the pipe. Let me call him."

74

I called him, and Eduardo said, "He had to get back to Atlanta; he had something important to do.

I interrupted him quickly and said, "I'm sorry, dad having running water is not important?

"No," he said, "It couldn't be helped.

"I'll be back in the morning."

I said, "Around what time?"

He said, "Around 1 pm." Now, it's 1 pm.

I said, "Ok, I'm off. I'll meet you down there." He gave me this dry ok.

At this point, I realized I had to stay with him to get anything done. I was appalled at all of this because he presented himself as such a great businessman. As always, I was trying to please my dad. I had a lot of pressure on me with still trying to get my nephew settled in with a new job. But I agreed to renovate Dad's home; therefore, I felt that I must deliver. No one forced me to do this, but me being the type of woman I was, my word meant something to me. As always, when it comes to my dad, I try my hardest to please him. Especially now, since it seemed like no matter what I did, he always had a problem with it.

He was always mad at me, and it felt like he didn't believe in me. He questioned everything money-wise. He would always joke behind his questioning and say things like, "Well, for all I know, you could be robbing me blind."

This offended me so much because my dad knew I wouldn't steal from him. I then showed him every receipt to show him the proof, but what was strange was we never had trust issues, but suddenly, he started repeatedly questioning my word and credibility. I asked him where was all this coming from?

Finally, I said again, "If you don't trust me, why are you asking me to do the remodel?"

He said, "Because I don't know how to handle business as you do, and I have no one else to help me."

Once again, when I said, what about Sidechick? He shocked me with his look, "She has nothing to do with my business concerning the house," he said. I didn't know what had happened, but something did.

I asked, "Why not?"

He answered, "Don't worry about it, just know she doesn't, and she doesn't know how to do anything like this anyway. I've told you before, the only thing she is worried about is Ma and any other woman that she thinks I'm dealing with."

I said once again, "So Dad, why are you dealing with her?"

He looked again with a blank stare and said, "I don't know, but I got to figure out how to get out of this mess. I just need you to let me handle it.

I said, "Dad, you can't keep saying the same thing over and over and not doing something to get out of this mess."

On the next day, I headed to Thomson around 1 pm. It was a Thursday, and the Home Depot delivery order was supposed to come that day. Although I had seen no receipts, I could verify the order, and thus, I took Eduardo at his word. This was a put-up or shut-up moment for me. If the materials didn't come, I was prepared to ask for a full refund of the deposit from Eduardo. I was not hopeful at all, and honestly, I was ready to show my dad that I was right all along. I assumed Eduardo had been there and had gone.

We were waiting on the trusses to be made and the other materials to be delivered, so there wasn't much he could do anyway. When I called him, he said that he still hadn't left Atlanta.

I exclaimed, "What!" He said he was on another job and hadn't gotten away.

I immediately called my dad. "Dad, Eduardo says he hasn't left Atlanta yet," I informed him.

Dad asked, "What am I supposed to do about my water?"

I said, "Call him."

I knew that my dad wouldn't call because my dad didn't like confrontation. He avoided it at all costs. Most times, he would walk away or avoid not to have to deal with things. Therefore, he wanted me to handle the renovation. He knew I did not play with people. I am firm, but I also know the game. I'ma get what I need done. I always negotiate, but I am also sturdy. One rule - Do what you say. That's it.

This was yet another reason why I didn't understand why he was in a knock-down, drag-out relationship with this woman. Because all they did was argue every damn day. He didn't tolerate it at all. Not from me or my sister, no one. He would walk away and act like he didn't know you. I just wanted to know what changed? Because maybe if I understood, I could accept the time he was asking for to remove this woman from our lives. But he could never tell me why.

At the beginning of the renovation, because I knew how our relationship had changed so drastically, I had to have a long talk about this very thing, and I made a lot of things clear, so there wouldn't be any problems.

I told my dad, "If you are going to let me do it, then let me do it. Don't give me the job and change the game, or else how are we going to do it midstream on me? I'll handle it all."

I also clarified that we needed to show a united front, no matter what, with no exceptions. If we decide together, it needs to stay that way in front of the contractors, so they won't see a sign of weakness from us and try to get over it. We agreed on everything. I oversaw the budget and who we hired. He would sit back and watch him forever home unfold. It was a moment to make him proud. Therefore, I didn't want any conflicts, especially in front of the contractors. He agreed and told me to handle it.

When it came down to him calling Eduardo, he still hadn't called when I made it to Thomson. I knocked on the door and asked him to come downstairs. I asked him why hadn't he called?

He said, "I decided to wait to give him more time."

"Why Dad?"

"Well, because he got more jobs to do besides mine."

I thought *if that's the case, why did you call me to complain to me about your water? Just keep on waiting on him and giving him more time. It's not like I have anything to do. You do what you think is best.*

I was officially over it. Finally, I guess he got tired of me complaining and called Eduardo because he wasn't there yet to appease me. Dad asked Eduardo where he was? He says he ran out of gas on Highway 120.

I told Dad, "I think we have made a mistake. Something doesn't sound right about this story. He keeps on giving me excuses and still hasn't produced one receipt or product. And, when I call, he doesn't answer but will call you back and give you excuses. He knows it doesn't work with me, so he will call you, Dad. And that isn't right."

Dad thought about it for a quick minute and began to get mad.

Then, he called him again and said, "You know Eduardo, Jen is right. I thought you would be more considerate of the fact that I haven't had water in my house all day. I need to get my water on very soon."

Finally, my dad had stood up to him. He finally listened to me after we had been waiting 3 hours. It should not have taken that long. Eduardo finally got to our home around 6 pm with the same excuse of the gas running out.

I asked him, "How? We just gave you 10,000 dollars for a deposit."

I learned a lot that day about jack leggers. They will beat you if they know they can. They will also speak to the weakest one making decisions because they feel they can get over it. But I didn't have it. I was no-nonsense. My dad was Mr. friendly, and Eduardo knew this. He was also the first contractor to teach me not to pay before seeing the work done. It was a great education for me. I have wanted to go into this business for over 20 years. I needed to know what to look for and who not to let slide.

Eduardo knew my father was the nice one that accepted no one's perfect approach, and he played on it every time he had another excuse. But I knew a con when I saw one. So, you had to wake up early to fool me. I told him that I was not having it anymore. So, CUT THE BS! I asked where he had been? He said that he was just cruising down I20, and the time got away from him.

I said, "I thought you were out of gas?"

He said, "Yeah, but that was when I was in Atlanta. I noticed he wasn't alone. He had some Mexican lady with him.

I said, "Did it matter to you that you had us waiting and my dad hasn't had water all day? This makes no sense, and you are being very disrespectful to my father."

I then asked again for the receipt for the materials, and he said, "I'm sorry, I left it at the office. I will send it as soon as I go back to Atlanta."

I asked where the delivery that was supposed to be there was?

He said, "He was notified that it was going to be delayed another day."

I told him that I didn't feel good about it. I asked if we could get our money back? He said, "No, we signed a contract. I'm here now and ready to do the work."

I said, "Dad, we have made a mistake. Let's get the money and find someone else." Eduardo was pleading with my dad while I didn't know what I was talking about. He pulled the 'You have to have patience in a remodel' card.

And my dad said, "You are right and ok; I'll give you another chance when the pipe is fixed.

He said, "I no longer want to work with Jennifer because of her bad attitude."

I said, "The only reason why you are saying that is because you are up to no good, and you know that my dad will allow you to do whatever you want." I watched him and dad laugh while talking about how men should handle things like this. I stood there feeling like a fool. He didn't do any work that day either, and when he left, I said, "Dad, I thought we agreed that we would not go against each other with the contractors?"

He said, "Jennifer, you brought him to me, and the first time he messes up, you want to fire him. Nobody is perfect. Are we not his only customers? And, we may have to work around his schedule."

I may not know much about contractors, but I do know the business, and that's not how this is supposed to work in any business plan where you have contracted someone for $30,000. You are supposed to be available for this job because you have a deadline. And, because he hadn't got started within two weeks, I pushed the deadline up two weeks to put a fire up under his tail.

I knew right then that my dad and I couldn't work together on this project. I believe in people's words. And at any time a person didn't keep their word with me, I was prepared to move on to someone who would have no problem with doing what they said.

Business is business with me, and if we are paying someone to do a job for us, there should never be a time when our needs are not being met, and we don't know what is going on. It was too much for me. I didn't understand a lot of things about this situation but, I knew it wasn't for me. It was more stress than I was willing to handle. And after multiple calls and emails, back and forth, for a couple more weeks and multiple excuses, there was still no product.

Eduardo sent me a picture one day around 4 pm saying he was at Ace Hardware in Thomson ordering the supplies. He made sure it showed the tools around him, and I was to the point where it was time to do something about this. I sent the demand letter and asked for the money back, or I would sue. Every day since he was supposed to start, there was an excuse or a no-show. He was supposed to be at Ace's picking up wood for the footing and any tools he needed. Yet, we never saw anything but a 2x4 and a screwdriver.

When I constantly threatened to sue, He stopped answering and didn't answer me at all. The only way he answered was if I called from another phone number. It was clear to me that he was exactly what I said from the beginning – a Con artist. My efforts were hindered due to my father allowing him to give excuse after excuse about why there were no materials. I got tired of arguing with dad about it.

I finally said, "You handle it."

I found a text on my phone between Eduardo and me, and he had given me the name of the company that made the trusses. I called them, and there were no orders; there were no orders at Home Depot. This man just took the money.

And, all this could have been prevented if my dad had listened to me and not had given him the money or at the very least requested it back. He was fighting me instead of listening to me.

After six weeks of arguing with dad, Eduardo told him that he didn't want to work with me because I had a bad attitude. Oh, that's another tactic the con artist used; paint me as the bad one. I was so angry with him and Dad that I let him work my dad. I played the background and literally stepped out of the renovation.

When Eduardo finally stopped answering any of our calls, Dad called me and asked what I would do because now Eduardo wasn't answering his calls either. I said what I had been trying to do for the last six weeks; file paperwork to get your money back. That is all we can do at this point. You wouldn't listen to me, and now, we are out of 10,000.

Once again, he said, "But you brought him to me."

And I said, "Yes, Dad, and when I realized my mistake, I tried to correct it, and you stood in my way. I am done with the blame game. The blame is on you."

I called the bank and they said there was nothing I could do for 90 days. I could place a stop payment on the check then, but the money may be gone by then. My only recourse was the court.

I was so angry that I had to come down again from Atlanta to file paperwork for something that could have been fixed. I was frustrated because, instead of fighting him, my dad chose to fight me. I was in such a foreign territory because I didn't know why. The only thing I could think it could be was the negative person he was sleeping with every night. Nothing made sense otherwise. Why else would you lose $10.000 when your daughter was warning you about this person. There had to be more to this story. There just had to be.

Chapter Eleven

My Mind State and My Glow

During the onset of the spell, I lost my glow. I've always had a distinct glow in the middle of my forehead. I always called it my beacon of light because it was so overwhelming, as if God Himself marked me. My glow always stood out to me in my pictures. Tell you what, if you review my old pictures on my social media between 2013 and 2016, you will see it too. There was a light there that was my happy light. It was as if God himself marked me with this distinct light that shines to represent him. But, when I noticed the change in me when I noticed my mental state of confusion and always being unsure of myself, I noticed the light was gone. Sometimes, now I see the glow again, but it's faint and not noticeable as before. That is just another reason how I know I've changed.

These people tried to take my mind and would have succeeded if only I hadn't been smart enough to figure out what was being done to me. I didn't really know that I was under a deadly spell until I met Michelle on that day. If she hadn't walked up to me and asked if I read my bible, I would still be lost, probably in a mental institution or dead. I was clueless and walked round in daylight with a flashlight. But I knew something was wrong. No one had to tell me. I was different. I knew that. But after my visit with Michelle, it all started making sense to me. And it became my reason for living. I was determined to beat them at their game. Whatever it took, no matter the amount of money it would take, I had to help my dad and me. I had to save him too. Because there was no way I could get whatever was done to me off me and leave him in misery with this bitch. There was just no way.

But now, since Michelle had moved and left the state? Who could help me? I talked to a local root doctor here in Thomson, and she told me to get some two things to take, and it would be off me. The only thing it made me was sick to my stomach, and once again, I realized that I needed help. There were so many rules don't talk on the phone about it because spirits carry it, don't tell anyone what happens when they are helping you to get rid of it because it will come back. So many rules, yet no solution. This drove me crazy, not figuratively, but literally; I was running around asking people what to do. They were giving me the names of people who lived in Warrenton, Atlanta, and South Carolina. I've always heard horror stories about South Carolina and how people traveled near and far to go get either roots taken off them or put them on someone. But, once again, I didn't really believe it. 'Cause, I felt it would never happen to me. But it did, and now I'm here running around obsessed to know what it was and how to remove it.

The final thing that the roots did to me made me unbelievable. No matter what I told someone, I was always misunderstood. I was always questioned as if I was lying. No one believed me when I told them things. It's like my words meant nothing to anyone. I argued with the guys I was dating. They didn't believe me. My family didn't believe me when I told them this woman had done something to me. My dad didn't believe anything I said to him. No one listened to me.

I was the pillar of my family, and pretty much everyone listened to me and my instruction because they trusted my words and solutions. My mom was supposed to be the matriarch of the family, but I guess since my dad had gotten custody of us, we became a separate entity, and I was forced into the matriarch role. In previous chapters, I spoke of how I was the one everyone, including my father, depended on, although it was very taxing on me. I was strong and could handle anything that needed to be done. I earned my respect with my family day in and out, and when they wouldn't believe me that something was wrong when I came home in 2016. They knew that I was different, physically and mentally. They said that I had become mean and disconnected. I appeared different mentally because I couldn't figure out things so quickly anymore. I seemed confused most time and seemed lost. I stopped taking pictures because I thought I was ugly; the list goes on and on but, it made them question my mental state.

I didn't dress the way I normally dress. Hygiene was void. I simply didn't care how I looked at all anymore. I didn't care about fashion or makeup anymore. Anyone who knows me knows that I am a Diva, yet I didn't want to dress up anymore. It wasn't a big deal to me as my family noticed the changes in me. I was fighting inside and outside, screaming at them that "She did something to me. She did something to me", but they would not listen. They didn't believe in roots, i.e., my dad and daughter.

They didn't believe in roots, which means they didn't believe me, but that was also the way this spell was designed to take away all my credibility. It made me seem as though I was crazy. And no matter what I said or did, the people who knew me, even the people who were not my family and knew me, would question the validity of my claim.

No matter who I told, they always tried to make it seem as if I just didn't want my dad with this woman. I would talk about the constant arguing and accusations this woman was always throwing at dad. I would talk about the furniture and what she did to it. It was always just let your father be happy. I would talk about the house's unexplainable smells, which everyone just brushed off. I would show them my back. Their reaction was always, "you sure?" I would tell them about what Michelle told me about the spell and who did it. I told them she described this woman to a tee. People were intrigued but always came to the question of *how many women has your dad put around you? Or why are you so obsessed with this woman? Or you just miss your dad, don't you, and you don't want another woman in his life.*

But that was the farthest thing from the truth. I loved Ma, and she was a woman, so why didn't I have a problem with her. These were crazy questions to hear from people, but once again,

91

that's the way it was designed. The only thing that everyone was in a consensus about was if I would say, "Do you see that I'm different?" The answer would always be yes. But no one would believe that this woman had done anything to me, and one time even, I had a friend who asked me if I was on drugs. Drugs, no, I smoked weed, but I would never go any further after losing my marriage to cocaine. So, that wasn't it, but what was causing me to be so different and lose my credibility with my family and others.

Imagine being a pillar of success and trust, but now I was reduced to a lying, dysfunctional mess that no one believed in anymore. And the biggest part is not understanding why it was done.

She could have done anything else to me but, why roots? I felt because it was the only thing that she could use to get to me. I'm way too smart for anything else. My bed was used to destroy me. Whatever she placed in my bed entered my back, and from what I'm being told, a tree began to grow.

During those five days, I was bound to my bed. Unknowingly the spell was completed. This explains the wood coming out of my back when my daughter tried to bust the bump and the snakelike cyst coming out of my back. And the loss of my glow and the loss of my mental state. But, why roots? All because I love my dad and want the best for him. All because I want him treated right. All because I cared about who was around him and what they were doing to him. No, it had nothing to do with that.

I couldn't understand why this woman hated me so much that she would go to these lengths to get me hemmed up, as they say. But she did it, and it just didn't make any sense to me. I was in a foreign land. And, although I didn't know what exactly was done to me, I knew who had done that to me. Now, I had to prove it. And that was going to be the hardest thing. Where was it? I saw that my words meant nothing to anyone anymore, I concluded, I had to come up with evidence that it confirmed what I had been saying all along when you saw it. I had to find it. I felt it had to still be in the house. But Where was it? It's still got to be somewhere in the house, I thought. I desperately needed the evidence to prove I was right. I began searching for it in the house. I started checking the attic, the vents, the mattress, and everywhere you could think after tirelessly looking over and over my dad's house, my old room, his room. I stopped and thought, *what was I missing?* It had to be somewhere close to me.

And then it hit me. I heard Michelle's voice just as plain as day. "They entered you through your back." I realized that it was still inside of me, I broke down.

It had to be still at work because why was I still getting sick every time I went into my father's house? Why were we arguing instead of being the way we have been our entire life? I was so confused and lost. And I finally felt this thing was going to kill me.

This spell was cast on me to make me lose my mind, confuse me, make me second guess everything I ever knew, make everyone question me, and debilitate my body. And now it was succeeding, but only on my left side; why? This spell was also to prevent me from ever being happy again in love or life.

When it started in 2016, I had no idea what it was; I just thought I was in Menopause. But menopause couldn't make me sick from a smell in a house; menopause couldn't put a snake-like cyst in my back; menopause couldn't do all this. At least that is what my mom told me because she too was forced into menopause early due to fibroids. So, menopause wasn't the culprit. This was more; this was evil.

My gut was telling me that I was right, and this wasn't normal. It had nothing to do with my medical health. This was all mental, and I was losing the fight to save myself. Also, concerning my love life, it seemed like no man that I had ever known or been with or even was conversing with me when this started wanted anything to do with me. No one called. It was almost as if I had died. My phone used to ring off the hook religiously with wanna be's, yet no one called me after the onset of the roots at all in 2016. No one which I encountered looked at me the same. I used to be the star of the room, and now, Men always looked away, which took me further down a dark hole. I was losing my self-confidence, I began losing my ability to talk effectively. I began to lose everything.

Chapter Twelve

I CAME HOME
Mid 2018

As I continued my life in Atlanta, I had made up my mind to
continue the renovation. We didn't give Eduardo all the money.
So, we could keep working, next was the kitchen. My dad had
lived in the house with a hump on his kitchen floor. My next
project would be to get the kitchen floor fixed and the dining
room floor to make them all leveled. I just couldn't believe my
dad had let the floor stay that way. But it is just dad we are
talking about. All he ever did was gamble and was hardly ever
home. He didn't care whether he had a roof over his head or not.

I continued to travel back and forth to Thomson. I also kept
trying to contact Eduardo, yet I knew that the money was long
gone, and the only way to get it back was through the court
system. I went to Gwinnett County to file the paperwork for

them to tell me that he lives in Gwinnett County, but the actual theft had happened in Thomson, Ga. Therefore, I would have to file it where the crime principally occurred. The next day, I went to Thomson and filed theft by taking charges against Eduardo. I was told that it would be very difficult to pursue Eduardo because he lived in Atlanta, but the paperwork would be sent there, and if he was arrested, they would have to hold him and extradite him back to Thomson.

At this point, it was all I could do for my dad. I was so angry at him, but I always kept in the back of my mind that he was not my dad. He would speak rudely to me and would often argue too. Because she was always using him to carry her message, she was angry at me, because I didn't accept her. I clung to Ma because she was real. This woman was nothing compared to her, and she knew it. No matter what she put on my dad, he never left Ma alone. He called her repeatedly in front of her, and it killed her for me to ask him about Ma in front of her.

She knew, what he wanted, and he didn't want her. She had to root him up for him to be with her while she had nothing going for herself and I saw it. I would know when she accused my father of sleeping with us. I usually don't grin away stuff like that because it's wicked and evil. But I never accepted her; if anything, I was a threat to her future when I came home. I remember Dad called me, and my uncle Bo had a doctor's visit. Just so she could make sure my aunt overheard her trying to be nice to me.

She said out the blue, "I bet Jennifer knows."

First off, Heifer, no one calls me Jennifer. Sidechick, I don't like you, so why are you talking to me? So, please stop embarrassing yourself. Team Ma all day! I continued talking to dad.

She once said, in her country voice, "Ask Jennifer, how do you know it's a Real Gucci?"

I was sitting there looking through the phone at dad like, what the f! I said Dad, tell her I don't know. I knew but didn't care to tell her. I didn't like this woman at all. She had a nasty spirit, and her mouth was reckless. She called and cursed my dad out one day about a screwdriver.

He answered the phone, and she asked, "Bobby, you got a screwdriver?"

He said, "No."

"Fuck you Motherfucker!" She shouted over the phone.

"Look, what do you want?" Dad asked, a bit annoyed.

"A screwdriver." She responded.

They argued for about 5 minutes about when he was coming over there, and he told her quite patiently, "Look, Sidechick, I'll be over there when I get there."

When my dad finally got off that phone, I asked him, "Dad! She did all that over a screwdriver?"

"She isn't right in the head. She had a bad childhood," he tried to explain.

"Dad, stop making excuses for that woman. She is crazy. And the way she talks to you is so disrespectful. A screwdriver, really!" I said gallingly.

This had become a daily thing. On every trip and time, this woman would call and argue all day with my dad and want to know his location and who was around him. When I came home to meet the people that would be doing work on the house Dad, and I would always be around him when she called. It wasn't like it was planned; it just happened that way. That is because she called on an average of 10 to 15 times a day from 1:30 pm, estimating when my dad got off to 10:00 pm. She would call, and he would answer her every time.

Every time he picked up her call, she would be saying, *where are you at Bobby, what are you doing Bobby, who over there Bobby* and on repeat, "Answer me, Bobby!"

And my dad would answer the questions half-assed until he got tired of her asking the same old questions, is what he called it.

"Look, Sidechick, I have had enough," he would say, and they would continue to go back and forth. And every time, he would say, "Well, let me get on out of here."

And then he would spend the nights in the projects. I just shook my head. The house was spotless, though, when I came home. She could easily pass for a maid as she cleaned that house like it was nobody's business. And that's the only thing good I could ever say about her. She was never there when I visited because she was not welcomed. Not after the incest comment, she had made and destroyed my dad's furniture. But I couldn't stop my dad, it was his house, and he wasn't listening to me, nor was he willing to. And the time I complained about the smell or the craziness of the relationship, he would shut me down and say, "I just don't like her and don't want him with her."

I would say you are right. I never hid how I felt, especially since I knew what she did to me. I just kept trying to convince my father to believe she did. I wasn't going to give up on that, but I saw myself losing the fight on many occasions. But still, I kept trying. Because giving up would cause me to lose my dad.

When my dad came home after being at Sidechick's house, he smelled like that horrible musty musk that she wore. It was like it was all over him, and now, it was in his bed and room too. Anytime he had the smell on him, I made it my business not to touch him in any way. There was something about this smell, and whatever it was, it controlled him because he acted differently as if he was a zombie. And I knew this was the key to the spell he was under.

I saw my dad getting closer to Sidechick. He was taking her around my aunt and uncles, and they were going back and forth to the doctors with my aunt and uncle and always having lunch or dinner together. She was the first woman that my dad took around my family other than my ma. When I found this out, I asked my dad what was he doing?

"You never take sides around the family so, why now?" He made up so many excuses to me. "She helps me drive to the appointments."

"Oh, so she is driving now. When I first met her, she was a nervous wreck, but now she driving?" I knew this was a game she had been playing the whole time.

"Yes, she feels comfortable enough to drive by herself now." He said.

"I am just taking her around them to make her feel accepted since you don't make her feel that way." He said in a complaining tone.

"Dad, there is no way I will ever accept her. But, for you to have her around the family, What about Ma?" I said.

"Just don't mention anything to her about Sidechick, please," Dad said in a sheepish tone.

All I could do was shake my head because dad didn't know. I was already telling Ma everything that was going on. After Sidechick called Ma and said what she said to her, she reached out to me. I told her the truth and that my dad was staying in the projects every night. She wasn't shocked at all because this woman was like number 2586, as it seemed. She was used to him playing around. But she couldn't understand why he lied to her when she asked about this woman. He never claimed this woman to her, never admitted a thing. When she would tell my dad that her family and other people from Thomson were telling her what was going on, my dad would deny, deny, deny, and would always say he didn't even know this woman. But he was lying every single time. Once again, it didn't make sense.

As I continued to work for Xfinity, I began dating a guy I worked with named Kwamee. I knew it was a mistake from the beginning because he was dating another girl who we worked with named Shontae. There was something about this guy that intrigued me. He was a sexy being that I could not get enough of, no matter how much I tried. When we first began to mess around. He would always make it seem as though Shontae was so in love with him, but he didn't feel the same.

I didn't care; however, I just wanted love and affection from anyone at this point. Because, as I said, no one was showing me any attention, which was very odd. He was the first one to show me attention in a very long time, and I fell for it. I didn't like Shontae anyway because of her attitude. So, sleeping with Kwamee didn't bother me at all. But why would I do this?

I knew relationships at work are the worse relationships you can have, but I couldn't help it. I was so lonely, desperate and vulnerable that I wanted something to fill the void I had when it came to men. I hadn't been with a man in months, and I just wanted to feel good for once. I just wanted to feel wanted because, as I said, no man would touch me or look at me.

I finally broke down to Kwamee's advances and gave him a chance to see me. We started dating and going out, and at first, it was so much fun. We would lay around and talk about Shontae and him. He would make it seem like she was a paymaster, and he didn't want that from a woman. I just ate it all up and kept on digging my claws into him as we continued to see each other for months. I was still having problems with my nephew and was trying to get his medicines regulated. I went to several doctors, but nothing seemed to work.

He was still falling, and I didn't know if it was from all the meds that the group homes had given him or if it was due to the traumatic brain injury he suffered. But I wasn't giving up. I was determined to help fix him, no matter what it took. He had been through too much in his life when he wasn't even responsible for it. He didn't deserve it.

Kwamee was so involved with him and his progress. He would call and check on him every day, keeping me encouraged that he became my rock to depend on. But it didn't last long. After about three months, Kwamee changed suddenly and began falling back from me. He stopped calling every day, and he wasn't even coming over like he used to. And, when I asked what changed and why he stopped seeing me the way he was, he couldn't give me an explanation. It seemed that he and Shontae were getting closer, and I couldn't understand it because he always negatively spoke of her. She was very much in love with him, and it seemed as if he was falling in love with her.

"It's like she is obsessed with me, but I don't feel the same way." He would always say.

So, what was drawing him closer to Shontae and not me? We were spending so much time together and had become quite close, and I loved the attention he was giving me at home and at work. But as I said, he stopped, and we hardly saw each other outside of work at all. I would come to work, and we would speak to each other, and I watched him and her playing around in the break room, and it seemed as though he was flaunting it in my face. I could not tell myself why he didn't feel the same way for me anymore. I could not figure out how he could pretend we were not together at all anymore. And I was more shocked when we finally talked, and he told me the reason why he didn't want to mess around anymore.

"It's not that I didn't want you because I still do but, there is something that keeps you on my mind, and it is not a good thing," he said.

"What do you mean?" I asked, stunned.

"No matter what I do when I pick up the phone to call you when I get in my car to come to see you, even when I think of you. Something says to stay away. It's almost like a voice that tells me to stay away from you, and it scares me." He tried to describe.

"Stay away? Voice? What?" I could not understand a word.

"Yes, stay away, and every time I try and fight it, something happens to me to stop me. I didn't understand it but, I did." He had said.

Something is at work to make sure I was not happy in love or happy period. For the first time in months, I found someone that I really liked, and although the circumstances were out of the norm, I was sharing a man. I felt that I was not going to let go because this man was the first man in months to show me love.

I remained quiet at work or when I had to work with him, and he made it a priority to stay away from me. I clearly saw it and how he acted towards me, but I had to do my job. Then one day, I received a text from a coworker named Ausa. I noticed that Shontae was acting differently towards me as well. She didn't speak or talk to me like she used to, and I felt she may have known what was going on between Kwamee and me. She would make slick comments about Women and how they should get their own man around me. I ignored it and thought, *if she wanted to know what was going on, she could ask me directly.*

106

Because I didn't know if she knew, I didn't even care, but at the same time, I also was so confused about the sudden disconnect between Kwamee and me. I had so many other things going on, with my nephew, running back and forth to Thomson during the renovation and trying to get myself back mentally up to par because something was messing with my head. When I received a text from Ausa, I knew she was up to no good. She asked whether there was something wrong.

"No, why do you ask?" I questioned her instead.

"Because you seem different. Has someone done something to you that we work with? She seemed concerned about me.

"Ausa, if I speak on what was done, it will cause problems, and I don't think anyone wants problems here. I'm good, thank you." That is all I said to her.

She further followed up with, "Are you having a problem with Kwamee?"

I was like, "Where did that come from?"

"Well, Shontae saw texts between you and Kwamee and wants to know what is going on?" She directly came to the point.

I then asked, "Ausa, what are you doing? Why are you asking me about Kwamee? Kwamee and I have been friends for a very long time. We normally text and call each other. We work together; therefore, there may be text messages. It doesn't mean we got something going on."

I thought by me denying it, she would just let it go, but the following day. Shontae confronted me about Kwamee. And all hell broke loose. It was the way she came and stood over me and said, "I want to talk to you."

I didn't want to lose my job. I had benefits and a good pay salary there, and I needed that for both my nephew and me, but I wasn't going to let her disrespect me.

I stood up and said, "About Kwamee?"

"Let's go to the back and talk," I told her quietly.

When we got to the back Kwamee was there already.

"What is going on with you and Jen?" She asked.

Kwamee said nothing.

"She will not leave me alone. I tried to tell her that I was done, and she won't stop."

"What?" I went off on Kwamee and said, "What in the hell are you talking about? I haven't spoken to you in months on a personal level. I watched your actions, and that told me everything I needed to see. Although I didn't understand it, I accepted it. Therefore, you and I have nothing going on."

Shontae, stood there and watched and silently listened and finally said, "I want to know what was going on?"

"We were friends, and he said he didn't want you, and the only reason he was with you is that you do his work for him."

"Jen, I told you that in confidence."

"Yes, you did but, you are not gonna make it seem like it was all me alone." Kwamee got mad.

Shontae and Kwamee started arguing, and the manager Anthony came into the back room because he heard all the commotion and wanted to know what was going on.

I was angry at the moment, and I said, "Somebody better get this girl!"

I knew it had something to do with the text from Ausa the previous evening. Why would she text me all out of the blue asking about Kwamee and me? Shontae started to throw insults about me being too old and why I wanted someone else's man? I knew I was wrong but, I couldn't let her insult me.

As I said, I didn't like her, but that wasn't it. I was so desperate for someone to show me love, and Kwamee did that for me. I didn't care what she thought of me. But Kwamee was the one I was angrier at because of the way he tried to play me. It was as if I was the only one who was trying to get with him. We had been seeing each other for three months, and now, when he got caught, the only way he could find a way to fix things with her was to deny me and accuse me of chasing after him. 'Typical guy,' but it made me angrier that this was the only way he could tell the truth.

The manager took us into the office because the argument was getting louder and louder. We then went into the office and talked about what just happened, and I told the manager and Shontae that I had been seeing Kwamee for the last three months, and I guess Shontae just found out. After we went back and forth a few minutes, Shontae stormed out, and I sat with Kwamee, and the manager went behind Shontae.

"I'm sorry, I didn't have another choice. She saw the text message we sent each other the other night and threatened to make me lose my job if I didn't stop seeing you." He apologized.

"Kwamee, we haven't seen each other in months. There was no reason for you to confirm anything about us. I accepted it and moved on, and now all of this because, of what?" I asked him, looking straight into his eyes.

He couldn't explain to me why this transpired, and I got even more upset. Because now everyone knew what was going on with us. And, I looked as though I was wrong and messing with someone else's man. Shontae stayed gone for hours, and the tension and gossip trail kept growing at my job that day. It was hard but, I continued to work, and after my shift, I went home. Around 10 pm, I had a knock on the door. It was Kwamee; he was apologizing and trying to explain what happened and how he was so sorry.

"I want to keep on seeing you, but as I said, something just isn't right." He said, again, "Every time I think of you or try to see you, something happens to me. On my way over here, my car shut off repeatedly but, I finally made it to say to your face, I am sorry, and I want us to continue to be friends." He sounded desperate, but I was not willing to make myself a fool again.

"There is no way we can remain friends. I need to figure out what I need to do concerning work because there is a 0% no tolerance for employees having relationships at my job. I didn't think I would get in trouble because they were seeing each other too. Therefore what we were doing shouldn't be that big of a deal. If they didn't get in trouble, why would I? I was still worried, though, because I could lose my job, and I really need it to keep a roof over my and Lagearld's head." There was no way I was holding anything back.

"Why did you show her the message anyway?" I really wanted to know.

He told me that she had taken his phone all of a sudden. He once again apologized to me before leaving for telling her I was after him. That same day, I started receiving text messages from an unknown number, and they were saying all kinds of crazy things to me. I responded at first with equal amounts of badass. Then I realized it was a woman, and it was Shontae. The next few days were hard to work because I knew this girl was texting me. I went to management and showed them the text messages, and they talked to her but did nothing about the situation. While Kwamee avoided talking to me, he sent me a text to meet him out in the back. When I got to the back, he and Shontae were both there. And I guess it was confrontation time, and I was all for it.

Kwamee, started with "Why are you lying on me?"

"What? Um, Kwamee, what are you talking about? I spoke to management and told them the truth, and now, I'm getting harassing text messages, and it is all because of you."

I kept watching Shontae move closer to me, and I stepped back just in case.

Kwamee said, "All I got to do is say the word and... I looked at them both and began walking into the building. I asked to leave to get a restraining order on them. I felt unsafe and would not return to work until this matter was settled.

I finally went back to work a week later as I was assured nothing would happen to me. I was still getting the harassing texts and still felt unsafe and contacted HR. After HR was contacted, I went back to work for a day and was contacted by a detective on my case. He told me the address I gave him was not the correct one. And he could not serve the restraining order unless I had a new one. I remembered Kwamee had an account. I made the conscious decision to look his account up and gave the detective the address. About two weeks later, I went to court on the restraining order for Kwamee only because since Shontae didn't say anything, I couldn't get one on her. As we were in the court, Kwamee, Shontae, and Kwamee's mother were there, and I was showing the judge the text messages, explaining what had happened, and the judge laid into him.

"I cannot believe they didn't know where these text messages came from," the Judge said.

She told me she couldn't give me a restraining order because they were clever enough not to use their phones. But she advised me to make no mistake and that she believes me. And, she had a deputy to escort me all the way to my car. The next day I refused to go back to work until I was either transferred or they were gone. I finally went back to work for a meeting, and HR called me in the office. They fired me for accessing Kwamee's records. I got victimized all over again. These people were threatening my life, and I had to do something. But I made the wrong choice, and that was no one's fault but my own. I just felt so helpless; no one in the management or HR department seemed to take this seriously. It almost seemed like they hated me for it. From the onset of the confrontation in the store till now, absolutely no one talked to me. Maybe, just for business, but no one even spoke to me. The Managers had no choice, but they treated me as if I had the plague. So, I felt justified in my actions and caused myself to get fired. I applied for unemployment, and the managers turned on me. I lost even though they knew I was telling the truth, and the HR approved them to say it. Strange huh? I felt so defeated. How and why would managers and HR turn on an employee who was being bullied, who was being threatened, who was being harassed, and her life being threatened?

Bad luck just seemed to follow me, and all kinds of weird things were happening to me that made no sense at all. I was so confused and just waited for the next blow. Then, I lost my house as I couldn't pay the rent, and my dad wouldn't help me when I asked him. He straightaway said no. It seemed like bad luck was following me. Everything that could happen to me happened. I had two car wrecks back-to-back, I hydroplaned once, and T boned a car while it was turning.

Luckily they were found responsible because they turned. I was arguing with everyone about everything. I created a lot of enemies, and the sad part about it was, I couldn't help it. It was the only way I was and, I wasn't doing it. I was mean as hell to everyone. I was aggressive and, at most times, didn't have to be. My soul was suppressed, and I couldn't get free from what had me. I would try and fix my attitude but, I never could. That is another way this spell had control of me to destroy me. I was miserable, desperate, and had no male companion to help me through it.

I finally was able to reach Michelle, and she had moved to Savannah. She asked if I could come down, and I told her about me losing my job and my dad being potentially sick. I may need to move back home. She told me to go to him.

"She is doing something to him. You are the only one that can save him. If you can't come down, I can't come up until a couple of weeks but, go to your dad and save him. These women are evil." Her voice was powerful as she said that.

This phone call scared me. This woman told me what was going on with my dad and me, which made me not believe she was warning me again and I should listen. Right after I made that call and was just numb in fear, my dad called me and told me about his potential for prostate cancer. I still didn't know if I should go back home, considering what I already knew. I could wash the walls every time I smelled the horrible musty musk but, what about the house itself? I knew I needed to be home because if it was prostate or anything, I wanted to be close. But I knew it would be a war with this woman over my dad. I could not be around her; I could not see her, and every time I watched my dad go out that door, I was afraid he wasn't coming back that time. I didn't want to live like that anymore. I always feared for my dad's life because of how jealous and insecure this woman was, not to mention crazy.

Reflection: I remember my dad telling me a story about this woman calling him at work and saying she was following his truck, and she saw he had a woman in it, and if he stopped, she was going to kill them both. These were the horror stories that

116

my dad would tell me. Or, she threatened to kill Ma if he didn't stop seeing her. This woman was hideous with her threats, and I believe she meant every one of them, which is why I put nothing past her.

As I considered going home and what the cost would be to my already diminished capacity and mental state due to the spell., I partially decided that I could stay in Atlanta and find another job. I had been in cellphones for about 25 years. Therefore, I was sure I would find something. I really liked my life now in the aspect that I was away from my dad and could breathe. But I was especially glad I didn't have to deal with my dad and her. Dad was so far gone with this woman, and all he seemed to do was treat me mean and not want to talk or deal with me anymore. I didn't want to deal with that, but the fear of prostate cancer had put things into a different perspective. He was my father, and although I did not want to go, I ought to go. I do. In my time of considering what I should do, I was awakened every night by Michelle's voice, "Go to your dad. You are the only one that can save him."

And that's when I called my dad and asked him if I could come home. He then asked me whether I could find somewhere else to go. And I argued with him and asked why I couldn't come home? I needed to be home in case something else happened to him, and I wasn't even trying to hear of me going somewhere else to live. After that conversation, I stopped speaking to my dad because it was obvious who was pulling the strings. What woman would tell a man that his child can't come home to care for him unless she intended for it to be her? But how could she when she was the Sidechick.

As bad as my dad treated her, yelling, hiding , and never claiming her, she should have been glad he had someone to care for him. I was the only one of my father's children who cared about him. My sister is mentally challenged She only loves him because he is biologically her father. She feels as if she is forced to love him, and doesn't love as a dad. I am the only child that cared about my dad's wellbeing and the only one he trusted to care for him when he got older. Because he knew the other children didn't give a damn about him. So, it was bad enough that she was acting crazy about me coming home. But when dad told me he didn't know, and he needed to think about me coming home to my own home. I lost it. I had nothing else left to say to him. I was done. I didn't care about the renovation continuing because I made a good point. I was traveling every week for the renovation. I could just come on home and handle it from home. I thought it was a great idea till he shot me down. I blocked my dad and continued to look for a new job. I hoped he would be alright but I realized that he had just told me that I couldn't come home.

I never thought I would ever hear my dad say that since he built our house for this purpose and this purpose alone. It was her; she didn't want me home, because she knew it would draw my dad closer to my Ma. And she knew that was what I wanted, and I would pull my dad's attention from her. He listened to me. I had a lot of influence over my dad because I'm the one that had always been there for him, and he would do whatever it took to make sure I was happy, and that killed her. She hated me for it because she could never win against me. So, when I asked to move home, she stepped in and tried to prevent me from moving home.

(In previous chapters, I addressed this part, however, now I will tell you the whole story.)

But it didn't work. After two weeks, my dad called and left a message and asked me to give him a call. I really didn't want to call him back because I didn't want to argue anymore, I hadn't found a job yet, and my bills were coming due, and since I was denied unemployment from Xfinity, funds were getting low. I called dad back on a whim to see if he had come back to his senses, and he spoke and asked if I had found a place yet and if I had moved home?

"No, why should I? I have a home right there." I asked him, surprised.

"Have you tried the projects?" He asked.

I knew it was her then, because where does Sidechick live? The Projects. I honestly cursed my dad out that day. I knew the consequences of my actions, but I didn't consider him my dad because my dad would have never asked me something like that.

"You are with this woman, and she must be doing something to you. What in the hell are you saying to me? Don't call me anymore until you get some sense in your head. I am going to call Ma and tell her what you just said," and I hung up on him.

I didn't call ma. I cried first out of completely feeling betrayed, and not an hour later, my dad called me back and told me that I could come home. I fought him for a few minutes and then asked what was going on. I started sounding like a broken record. Because I had never gone through this before in my life, and combined with, I hadn't been able to get back to Michelle. I knew if I didn't get the help, this woman was going to take over, and I would have to fight her to get my dad back. I finally thanked him and hung up.

I then thought about the decision one more time. I did not have to go home. I knew I was in for a fight if I went back. I could stay in Atlanta and continue to live my life. I did not have to go home. But, yet again, when I went to sleep, Michelle came to me again and said, "Save your dad!"

The following day, I started packing up my things and went home. I rented a 26ft U-haul and friends helped me pack the truck. I drove it home with my car on auto transport. My ex-husband taught me how to drive 18-wheelers when we were married. I really didn't want to learn, but he said he wanted me to know how to drive if something happened to him. I hadn't driven one in a while, but the length of the truck and auto transport was the length of the 18-wheeler, and I handled it like a champ.

Just as I thought when I got home, he would have her visiting the house while I was gone. As soon as I got there, I began to smell the horrible musty musk smell. It was leading up to my dad's room. I knew she had been there or had just left. I remained quiet and started unpacking the truck with the help of my nephew and dad.

Every time dad came around me, I got lightheaded and kept trying to walk away from him, but sometimes couldn't be helped. I consistently felt lightheaded and sick to my stomach. I got moved in and slept on the mattresses that dad had on his old bed. The same mattresses that I slept on previously. The bed was already made up, so I didn't check the mattresses then. But when I woke up, I checked them just because I looked at them and still saw the stain from before when I slept. The greasy stain was still there, and I just stared at it and wondered what was greasy on my body to cause this stain.

I moved my bed in, continued using the mattresses, and tried to get settled in. After the first couple of weeks, I could no longer stand it. Every day around 2 pm, my dad would pull in after work and bring this witch to our home. He would come in, and she would be behind him, and they would go right upstairs to the room and stay until around 2 am. She wasn't allowed in our kitchen from the last time I was home and told her the directions to the stairs and the room. She would wear that horrible smell because she knew it bothered me. I told her before to stop wearing that stinking stuff to our house, so she was fully aware of how I felt about it. Especially since I knew that smell was for my father and me. It was there to make him love her and for me to get sick from the smell of it.

After she came one day at the beginning of the second week, I said, "Sidechick, I have asked you to stop wearing that horrible musty musk, it stinks, and I wish you would stop wearing it."

She looked at me with a smirk and walked upstairs. After that, I sat in my room for about 45 minutes and sulked to the point where I felt it was time to address this witch. And then I went upstairs and walked in and saw my dad and Sidechick sitting in a recliner and the Sidechick was in a cute, ill, old lady chair just staring at the tv.

I thought they were possessed at first, and then dad said, "Yeah, Jen?"

I said, "Dad, I need to talk to you. I don't feel comfortable here, and there is no way I am going to live here and be uncomfortable."

He asked, "What's wrong, Jen?"

I said, "I don't want this woman here in our home. She is evil and up to no good and she did something to you and me, dad. And I want her gone. I do not feel safe or comfortable in my own home and We don't want her."

Sidechick stood up, but I didn't move. I was sitting down beside my father and looking at her as if *Bitch, try it, I dare you,* and she said, "What's the problem?"

I said "You. And I am telling you, so no one else must tell you I said it. I know what you are doing, and I am your enemy, just so you know. I do not like you, and I want you to stay away from my kids."

She says, "I love those kids."

I said, "You love the fact that they are his grandkids and you will do whatever it takes to get to him. Stay away from my kids. Don't buy them anything, don't give them anything, and don't ever touch them again."

She said, "Bobby, You going to say something?" He just sat there and stared into space.

I said, "Dad, this woman is strange. Something ain't right about her."

She said, "Hmmm, that's the same thing he said about you."

I looked over at my dad in disbelief and said, "Dad, you are talking about me to this woman?"

Dad sat there and still stared into space.

"Why are you so insecure?," she said.

"I aint no damn insecure."

124

I said, "I can't tell, you are calling my ma."

She said, "I ain't called no damn ma!"

I said, "LIES, you called her cause you thought it would make my dad leave her for you, huh, you are a Sidechick, and as soon as you learn your place, the better you will be because Ma ain't going nowhere and neither am I."

She said, "We will see about that."

I didn't know what she meant but didn't care either. At this point, if she jumped, I would have killed her with my bare hands. That's just how much I hated this woman.

I told her also that she would never be ma. Ma has her own home and car; she doesn't live in the projects. She has worked her entire life. She does not get a crazy check. That's why she will never have my dad.

I ended it with, "He is my father, and you will never have him, especially since you would go to the lengths to hurt us. Dad take this woman home. We don't want her; we love Ma, and she will never compare to her. She is not welcomed in this house anymore, cutting up our furniture, calling people threatening them, and doing all this crazy shit all the time. We are a calm, quiet family. We ain't ghetto. We work for our stuff and try not to be destroyed. But, Sidechick, you better not cut another thing, and I mean that!"

She looks at me hard, like she is froggy.

I looked at my dad and said, "What do you have to say?"

He said, "Jennifer, I told you to let it go, and you won't let it go."

I looked at my dad and said, "Dad, this woman is trying to hurt me. And I don't want her back in the house. I don't feel comfortable in my home, and I can't stay here if she does."

I went to my room downstairs and heard my dad, and her go downstairs and leave. I felt a sigh of relief. He finally listened to me. I felt like I had stood up to the devil because that's exactly what she was - the devil. I thought the end.

On the next day, I walked around the house, and one of my neighbors stopped me to talk to me. She was excited to see me and said, "I haven't seen you in a while. How have you been?"

I said, "Well, I'm good. What's up?"

She said, "Can I ask you something?"

I said, "Sure."

She said, "What's up with your Dad? Why is he letting that lady yell at him and scream at him all the time, out in the yard,

126

and sometimes she screams so loud you can hear it through the windows and walls."

She said, "My granddad will tell you. He thought I was lying, and one day, he came around the corner and heard her screaming, and he told me that 'She is screaming at him.' I thought you were lying. Calling him all kinds of a cross-eyed son of a bitch, an ugly motherfucker, and no good ass." And, I said, "WHAT?"

She said, "Yes!"

I said, "When did this happen?

She said, "All the time, and I know Mr. Bobby don't let no women talk to him that way. So, something must be wrong with him."

I said, "Thanks so much. I've been in Atlanta. I didn't know none of this was going on. Thank you, and please let me know if you see or hear any of this again."

After talking to my neighbor, I slowly started to see why I needed to come home. Michelle was right. This woman was doing something real deal on my dad. If he was allowing her to humiliate him in his yard in front of his neighbors, my dad had lost his mind. There was no way. He was the King of his castle. He has the only house on the block and proudly boasts about it.

He always was a quiet, respectable, stuck in the 60's type of guy who liked peace. Everyone loves his sweet demeanor. But if someone took advantage of it, he let them and didn't correct them the first time.

My dad had two extreme moods. When he was sweet, he was all nice and loving. However, you better get out of his way when he blew because just as he was sweet, his other side was mean and nasty; he did not play. Especially if someone was trying to embarrass him, he would give you that look – The Crenshaw look, and you better get out of his face. But, this ghetto, overweight, out of shape and stinkin bitch out here in our yard cursing my dad out in broad daylight, and he hadn't checked her? I waited for my dad to return home from work after I heard this mess. I could not believe what I was hearing. He came home and went up the stairs. He was alone. I walked up to his room and asked if I could ask him a question?

He said, "Yes, go ahead."

I said, "Dad, what is this that I hear about Sidechick out here in the yard cursing you out, calling you out your name, and screaming so loud the neighbors can hear her through the walls of the house?"

128

He said, "She's angry, it happens, she accuses me of other women every day, every hour. I can't even look at another woman, or I get cursed out."

I said again, "WHAT? and you take it from her? Dad, what the hell is going on."

He said, "She had a bad childhood."

I said, "I don't care what she had. Have you lost your self-worth and mind together? You would never accept this from anybody, let alone a woman. Something is wrong here."

Once again, he said, "Look, Jen, let me handle it. All I need is another 10-15 years." I said, "10-15 years, yes, you have lost your mind? Who do you think will deal with this woman for 10-15 years when she has done all this crazy shit? Now she is yelling and embarrassing you in public? In your own yard? What has happened to you, Dad? Where is your mind? This woman is obsessed and very insecure and has damaged our property because of it. And you allowed her to come back to our home. Now, you are admitting to her yelling and screaming at you. Is she beating you, Dad?"

He laughed and said, "Naw, but she threatens me a lot."

I was livid. I said, "Dad, we can't take another year of this; you need to leave this woman alone."

Dad said, "I got this. I just got to figure out how to get out of this mess."

And, I said, "Dad, you are not doing well at that at all. It's time to act, not plan. You have now had five years, and ain't nothing getting any better. Get yourself together."

I knew that all that I had said to my dad was lost. Because instead of my dad agreeing with me, he was defending her as if this was normal behavior. She had cut up our furniture and carved her initials in our furniture. I didn't know the whole story but called a prosecutor and threatened to harm her about my dad, and then called my Ma to inform her about them. She accused him of sleeping with his children and cursed him out repeatedly in public, in his front yard, and a screwdriver, and was defending her at every word I said. I went downstairs and immediately called Michelle, and to my surprise, her phone number was disconnected. Lord, what am I going to do now?

I continued to think and ask anyone who would listen what to do. Every person said that she sounded like she had something on my dad. My girlfriend has always been the apple of my dad's eye. He will always be a ladies' man.

She came over to the house one day, and he stood at the top of the stairs and acted as if he didn't even know her. When others would see the change in him, it gave me relief because you start to question yourself if it's just you after a while. *Are you really losing your mind?* Because I knew my dad, and I knew that that wasn't the man that I was talking to every day. He even looked different to me at times. I would always watch him but never touched him. Until I got help, I wasn't taking any chances. But he wasn't the same. He even used her words and sounded dumb, just like her. It was painful to watch, but it confirmed everything I was saying to him and about him over and over. I was always the one who got the family together as I asked everyone when the last time they did anything with dad was?

I ran upstairs, and they were sitting in their chairs in the same positions staring at the TV. Everyone answered, "We don't see him anymore." I then came up with the genius idea to get all the family together to go out to dinner.

I said, "Dad, can we go out for a family dinner so you can spend time with your children."

He said, "No, Jennifer, I ain't going out with y'all?"

I asked, "Why not?"

He said, "Look, Jennifer, I know what you are trying to do. And I'll spend time with y'all when I am ready."

I said, "Dad, why don't you want to spend time with us?"

And then I said, "I know because she wants you to spend time with her all the time. But you have a family."

She said, "Bobby, I have told you. And I ain't going to tell you no more."

I said, "Told him what?"

She said, "I told him if he doesn't get you, I'm going to whip your ass!"

I said, "Well, I'm here and if you feel froggy leap bitch."

She said, "Bobby, you better get her."

I stepped out of my shoes and said, "As I said, I'm right here. What do you want to do because I have already told you? I'm his daughter, and I am home, and you won't have him. He has a family that loves him and Ma, and now you are threatening me? You really are crazy. Daddy, get this trick up out of here, and this time, don't bring her back."

My Dad stood up and shut the door. I waited and talked all kinds of noise, and then I finally went downstairs because I was ready to give her just what she had been looking for. She already had caused major problems with me and my dad, and the roots were just enhancing it to higher levels. It seemed like she wanted us to be always at odds to make her plan work. And I was ready to give her just what she needed; I wasn't the least bit scared of her and was prepared to show her what was needed too. I knew it wasn't over. That night was the beginning of my war, and I was ready. The nerve of her to threaten me to my father, and he did nothing. I knew I was on my own with this, but I never expected to fight my father to protect my father.

Chapter Thirteen

December 18, 2018,
The day I went to jail!

I could not sleep that night because I didn't trust this woman. She had threatened me for the first and last time. I had heard of all the people she was threatening or had threatened, and I was like she knows who to threaten. My dad brushed it off and made excuses for her, but I told him that night that she wasn't welcome in our house anymore. The following morning, I woke up and focused on the remodel. I had not worked on it since I had filed the charges on Eduardo. Since then, I had endured all of the foolishness with Kwamee and losing my job. At my home, I was drawing a blank and needed to recharge. Accompany that with dealing with my dad's situation, and I was overwhelmingly stressed. I had to get a crazy obsessive psychopath out of a house that wasn't mine and had to remove a spell that was cast on myself and my dad. I also had to find a job and provide income for my nephew and me, because I remember that although dad didn't say it, I was still responsible for paying something.

Lagearld and I were cleaning and unpacking still, and he yelled out to me "Nana, what is this?"

I walked into one of the guest rooms and saw a carving in this beautiful light brown wood dresser. An "SC" was carved in the wood. I absolutely lost it; Dad had told me about the initials being carved in it. I was really angry then and assumed they were new after I had told that demon, don't carve another piece of furniture. Oh, today she is not coming back in this house. I was so angry. I called my girlfriend, and she was listening and trying to tell me not to get in trouble. I had had it with all of this. This Bitch had carved the last piece of furniture. I waited for dad to come home on his lunch break.

When Dad got home, I was waiting.

I said, "Hey, let me ask you something," and I walked him into the guest room and said, "Do you know anything about this?"

He said, "Yeah, I told you she carved two desks and one dresser."

I said, "And you let her back into this house?"

He said, "Look, Jennifer, I told you to let me handle it."

I said, "Dad, it stops today. She will not come in this house again, and I mean it. Don't bring her ass over here today. I am going to whip her ass today if you bring her."

He said, "Jen, this is my house."

I said, "Well, she gon get her ass whipped today in your house, and I mean it. Bring her and see."

I was boiling. I got dressed, put on two layers of clothing, and my timz. I had cut my hair off because it was severely damaged. I dyed it a lot but still questioned everything. I had to determine if it was the way it should be, real, or caused by the spell. That was the hardest thing to do. Reality or Roots - that's what I dealt with daily, and the one who is causing my pain is coming into my house freely.

I was done. My blood pressure was so high. I was waiting on my dad to bring her back to the house. I knew he was going to say something, but I didn't know or care to hear. I got so angry to the point while I was pacing back and forth. I started calling and speaking to Girlfriend. She tried her best to calm me down. I could not hear her; I was so upset.

Standing up to me that way, my Dad lets me know he doesn't value anything anymore. He used to say, "Watch yourself, don't scratch anything, don't waste anything."

He was very protective of his stuff. He wouldn't even let me drive his cars. And he just acted as I had forgiven her, and it was alright. It's not alright. I was so angry; I walked to the corner store even though I had a car. It was as if I was possessed, and I was amping myself up higher and higher. I couldn't stop. I would not be satisfied until my dad brought this woman to our house. Today was the day that I was going to stand up to this woman who threatened me the night before, and I was going to win. I paced the half porch in front of the house. It had not been extended yet, so I paced it and waited, and right as he came in the driveway, I went and got a kitchen knife.

Reflection: I know why I picked up the knife. I was told that she was dating the guy that worked at a waffle house. And she stabbed him, and she is known for carrying knives, so I wanted to protect myself. She had a knife two nights before when she stood up. And I didn't fear her because I would stand up to her at all costs. Too much was at stake, and she cheated to win it by rooting people up. Win fair, that's what I told her. Win fair.

I started in a rage. I snapped, and I was ready for anything. I dared her to get out of the car. Dad kept saying, "Jen put the knife down."

I said, "No, I want this bitch to get out of the car."

My dad looked at me.

Sidechick said, "Take me home, Bobby," while unlocking the door; as she and dad wrestled with each other, I was going in on her. I called her all kinds of Sidechicks and low-budget project hoes and dared her to get out of the car.

My dad finally said, "No! It ends today." And he called 911. When I heard them say 911, what is your emergency? I snapped even further. My dad had called 911 on me. After, he brought the woman who threatened me the night before. What? I went off on my dad and told him to get his ass out of the car. How dared that he had called 911 on me. She asked if he needed the police.

He looked at me and stared and said, "Yes!" By then, I was daring them both. I accused her of the roots.

My dad replied, "Yeah, right!" I told him how he could do this to me. This is my home.

He said, "It's not your home." To hear him say that after I knew what he did for us, I went up another notch.

I said, "You are choosing this low-budget project hoe who want a come up over your child."

You called the police on me, Dad? How dare you, and I am trying to protect you too. I didn't ask for this, I came home for you, and you betrayed me!

I didn't know what I was prepared to do next, and dad said again, "Put the knife down," as the police drove up. My girlfriend was calling me; I had called Ma, she was calling me. Everyone was calling to calm me down, but I wouldn't listen to them.

Ma was sending text messages, but no, I had to end this even if it hurt me. She had to go. My dad sat there with his foot on the brake the whole time. He could have easily backed up out of the yard, but he stayed there to show her he would stand up to me. I threw the knife down because I thought they could kill me because I was a black woman with a knife. He even set me up to be killed by calling the police on me. I spoke to the officer, told him I had the knife, and began to explain why I walked into the house and showed him the carvings and still was talking cash shit to the root working tramp. I told her, "I'ma get you," as the police were asking me questions.

I was going off, and the lead police officer said, "Mam, you are making it harder on yourself. Just keep on talking. I didn't care at this point. I'm still threatening this woman and saying, "I'ma get you and you too, dad."

He betrayed me. He said, "OK 1099 her." I was reaching for a cigarette.

I think I had smoked the entire pack in an hour and, I said, "1099 her, what is that?" and he told me to put my hands behind my back.

As they were cuffing me, I looked over and said, "Dad do you see what you have done to me?" I was looking at my dad, and that bitch shot a bird at me. I don't know, but I completely snapped to the point of no return. I could not believe it.

I was right. She was doing this to make me snap. She knew that even her presence would ignite my hatred. I am sure my dad had told her what was going on before she came there. So, I wouldn't be surprised if she didn't do something to cause it to happen.

I said, "Dad, she is shooting a bird at me behind your back."

He looked back and just shook his head.

I literally drugged the police officer and said, "Take me to jail, let's go."

I was still going off and had every right to. I was being arrested, and she was picking at me because she wanted me out of the way.

As I sat in the car, I calmed all the way down until I asked if I could talk to my nephew, and they wouldn't let me tell him what was going on. He was in the door and watched me in the back of the police car. She got out of the truck and went in the house with him as my dad had sat and talked to the police officers. I did not know what they were telling them.

I was ready to go because I knew I could get out that afternoon. I got to the jail, and they processed me, then they told me that I wouldn't be getting out till Wednesday because the judge doesn't come in until Wednesdays to post bonds. I started looking around at the people I was locked up with and was plotting on who to get close to so that I could be protected because I don't do well in jail.

I'm a big bad wolf, but jail doesn't suit me. Yes, I've been inside before but for a few things related to my ex-husband. But I'm not a criminal. I'm scared to death of jail. But I do know there are bullies in there. See, yet another thing this spell took from me was my ability to stand up for myself. When has anyone known me to stand down or second guess myself? When has anyone known me to let people walk over me? It was a constant struggle, confusion all around me all the time. They were arguing for no reason because nothing made sense that they were arguing with me about. And that was a lot of people. I'm not kidding. But I was cool, I just said I would have to make the best of it, and the first person I called was my child in what would prove to be the most difficult conversation I had to have with her. I asked her to get me out of there.

She said, "I am trying but, what is wrong with you?"

I said, "What do you mean?"

She says, "Grandpa said you threatened to kill them both and that he feared you."

I said, "Grandpa turned on me. And I really don't appreciate that, but I wasn't going to hurt him."

She threatened me last night, and I was answering. "This woman has roots on us, Tiga. And, if you don't see it, something is wrong."

She said, "I see you are different. I saw you and thought you were gay. You cut your hair off and don't wear makeup anymore. I thought you were a dike now. I don't know what to believe. The woman says "She is afraid of you, and grandpa says you are losing your mind."

I said, "T, listen, remember when you pulled that wood out of my back."

She said, "Yes, I said this woman put roots on us both, Tiga, I swear to you on your soul. She is evil, T, and that's why my appearance and I have changed. Have you ever seen me focus on one woman this much?"

She said, "No. Which is why I want to know what's wrong? Ma?"

I said, "Nothing is wrong with me, I mean not me. I haven't done anything but protect myself. He and Dad turned on me for this woman. She has something on him too, Tiga."

She said, "Ma, I don't know, It seems to me you are just trying to run grandpa's life, and he said he is tired of it."

I said, "Oh my god, T, not you too, not believing me."

She said, "Grandpa says you are different, and now he is afraid of being with you, and after all these charges, I'm wondering, are you on drugs or is something wrong mentally?"

I literally dropped the phone. I could not even get my daughter to believe me. She listened to what they said about me and instantly believed in them.

She said, "Sidechick says you are obsessed with her, and I'm starting to believe it too. You have to let Grandpa live his life."

I said, "After all I have told you my entire life. I do not lie on people, you know I don't, so if I say she did something to me, she did something to me. You saw the wood. You say I'm different. You are even questioning my sexuality based on me cutting my hair off? My hair was damaged, and you know I am strictly dickly. So, there must have been a reason for this change."

I swore to her on my grandkids that is how far I had to go to get my daughter to finally listen to me.

I said, "She is using that oil she wears on him. He is under a spell," and I finally told her what Michelle had told me.

She said, "I don't know, ma. I don't believe in this stuff."

I said, "T, I swear on my grandkids, it's true. When can you get me out of here?"

She said, "When the judge gives you a bond."

I said, "How are you getting me out of here?"

She said, "Grandpa is using the house."

I asked, "Oh really?"

She replied, "Yes, and call back because Grandpa wants to talk to you."

I said, "I don't want to talk to him, especially if she is still there."

She had yelled at him to come downstairs, and he started talking to me as if nothing had happened. I went in again on him and how he chose that woman over me, how he betrayed me and said that the house wasn't ours and that he had built the house for him. *How could you call the police on me, dad?*

He had said, "I just didn't want you to kill her and end up in jail."

I said, "Dad, you know I'm not lying about any of this; how could you?" I just hung up on him; I had nothing else to say to him and furthermore did not want to hear anything he had to say because he wasn't saying it in front of Sidechick; it didn't matter and could be untrue.

I sat there in my cell and thought about what had just happened and how I had put myself in this situation. But I would do it all over again to stand up to this witch. I cried a lot because I felt so betrayed by my father. The officer told me he was charging me with simple assault, which was a misdemeanor and, I didn't care. I just wanted my voice heard against this woman who was causing so many problems within my family. On the first night, I passed up on the food because it was horrible. I slept on a hard mattress bed, and my back was killing me. At first, I said I would try and sleep the three days away, but I couldn't because I was in so much pain.

The following morning, I was called to the front to meet the police officers to get my formal charges. I was charged with two counts of Terrorist threats and two counts of aggravated assault.

I said, "What?" after reading the charges. You said that I was only going to be charged with simple assault, and now, I'm being charged with four counts?"

He said, "Yes, you are being charged with four counts, two for Sidechick and two for your father."

I said, "but I never threatened to harm my father, so why am I charged for him?"

At the time, I had no idea what I said because I totally blanked out, so I just continued to cry and said, "I would never hurt my father, I would never hurt my father!"

Before the officer left, he said, "Ms. Sherman, I really didn't want to charge you but, you wouldn't stop, so I had to do something to stop you." He then said, "I thought you had never been arrested before," and he smiled and walked out the door.

I was so defeated and lost.

When I got back, I told everyone why I was crying.

I said, "They are saying that I tried to kill my father. I would never hurt my father."

This one girl knew the woman I was talking about and said, "Yes, I know her, she works roots and has all these candles always burning at her house. That is what she be burning them for."

Then she tells me about her hanging at the bootlegger house in the projects drinking beer all day and talking about how she got your dad wrapped all around her finger.

She said, "I knew about you before I even met you. She often talked about how you were a problem but won't be a problem for much longer."

I said, "Oh yeah, she really said that?"

"She has another thing coming because I wasn't playing with her today and will fight her for my dad. She told me to be very careful because she may try to put something down while you are here. She told me about how she made her husband sick, and he won't leave her alone. Sidechick is over his house every day, cooking and taking care of him," she said.

I was just looking in disbelief but she had a problem with any woman my daddy was talking to. This woman was so trifling and the first woman my dad ever let cheat on him, and he knew it. I went to bed that second night, knowing I would be out the next day because it was Wednesday, and I was so ready to go home and get a decent night's sleep.

The following morning, I went before the magistrate, and my dad, mom, and daughter were there, as the judge asked me if I had anything to say?

I said, "Yes, I explained how this woman had damaged our property and shouldn't be allowed back in our home."

I told him how the woman had threatened me the night before and had been threatening everyone around my dad. The judge preceded to tell me that this was my daddy's house, and I didn't have a right to tell someone they could not come to our house. If he accepted her destroying his property, I had nothing to do with it but accept it. I looked at the judge like he was crazy as I asked the judge to drop the charges.

He said, "I cannot drop these charges, but it seems to me they should have been two charges instead of 4? Mr. Crenshaw, what do you have to say about this matter? What do you think I should do about it?"

My dad says," Your honor, she didn't mean it, she was just upset, and I am asking you to let her go."

The judge said, "I will listen to you as her father gave me a $50,000 bond."

I went back to my cell and waited for my daughter to get all the paperwork together to get my property bond approved. I was calling her back-to-back because I was so ready to get out of that place. I had no idea what had been done at our home. I didn't know if this woman had done something else to me or my things which further put me into a disconnected state. I felt she had done something, and I needed to get some help to get rid of this woman.

I was released at 1 pm that day but wasn't processed out until around 9 pm. They take their precious time to let you out. I don't know if it is to teach you a lesson or what, but I was just glad to go home.

As I walked out of the jailhouse door, I saw my daddy standing on the other side of the door smiling and saying, "Hey baby, how are you. I got angry all over again but was glad to know that he still came to get me. We stopped by the door to get me some cigarettes, and we went home. He kept saying to me, "all I was trying to do was get you to listen to me."

I said, "You should have never called them, dad. You betrayed me in front of this skank and, I will never forgive you for it. I am going to get out of your house as soon as possible."

He then said, "No, you can't leave the house because if you don't go to court, I will lose my house."

I said, "What, in the hell did you just say to me?"

He repeated it, and I said, "Dad, so you think I would not go to court?"

He said, "I'm just trying to protect my house."

I said, "Dad, why would do you think I wouldn't go to court? You have known me my entire life. I would never not go to court to get a matter handled, so why would you say that."

He then says, "You know you are going to have a tough time since you have a criminal record."

I said, "Dad, who has a criminal record?"

He says, "From what I was told you do, and it's going to look bad when you go to court."

I said, "Dad, I don't have no damn criminal record; who told you all of this? The police?"

He said, "No, Sidechick said it to your aunt and me."

I told my dad, "So you are going to believe a dumb hussy over your own daughter, dad? I don't have a criminal record, dad, and I will go and move to any place I want. Because if you are saying, I can't leave this house to move somewhere to get peace. You have another thing coming. The nerve of you to listen to that dumb, stupid ass woman, and what's worse is that you believe her"

The betrayal continued, and I wasn't having any of it. We got home, and I went downstairs to my room and started looking around to see if anything was out of place. The only thing I noticed was the horrible musty musk smell that was now on my walls in the back of the house. This bitch was relentless, and there was no excuse for the oil to be in my area because it was separated from the house by a door that should have been locked while I was gone. But, due to the fact that I didn't have a chance to lock my things up, everything was free game, and I am not putting anything past her.

I asked my dad, "Why was this oil back on my walls?"

I told him, "She was trying to harm me, and you were helping her."

I began washing the walls with pine soil again. I was so tired of this situation, and now everything was deliberate, no matter how great or small. My dad could never tell me the reason the oil was placed in my section, mainly because he couldn't smell it, because he was always smelling it on himself. I knew I had to get out of this house. I couldn't even trust my dad, so I couldn't expect him to protect me.

I went to bed. My dad stayed home that night. I didn't know that it would be the last time he did stay home for a very long time. On the following morning, I was visited by Detective Black from the Mcduffie County Sheriff's office. I thought it was just a protocol visit and procedure. Detective Black was the scene who wrote up the charges after speaking with my father and Sidechick while I was in the police car. Still, I never knew what was said to him or the other officers when he spoke to those two.

I asked Detective Black, "How could I help him?"

He said, "I'm going to stick my neck out for you and ask you to come work for me."

I laughed. I looked at him and said, "Thanks for seeing who I really am."

At first, I really thought this guy was just coming on to me.

He said, "I understand you were upset, and you may have a right to be, but things happen. And I know if you are as good calm as you are angry, you can make a lot of money. You were just upset."

I said, "Well, Detective Black, if you know all of this, why are the charges still standing, and why do I have four charges vs. the one charge the officer told me I would have?"

He said, "Four?"

I said, "Yes. He told me to let him check into this and see what he could do."

I then felt compelled to attend a seminar for his marketing company. He invited me to a very prestigious hotel filled with people who were also with his company. There were teams, and he was the team-lead, and we sold life insurance policies. I introduced myself because I felt it spoke volumes for a police officer to come to me and ask me to work for him. I had so much bad luck and misfortune while standing up to this bully. Also, I wasn't my normal self and knew that I second-guessed everything. My confidence went down tremendously due to what was being done to me. I felt I was wronged, betrayed, and lost in this situation because no one would listen to me when I tried to tell them what was wrong. But, once again, that was how it was designed.

To cause confusion and disbelief. I was really burned out on sales. I had been in sales for 25 years, and I got tired of trying to convince people to buy things. It got to a point where my reputation was like; I just told them what they needed based on what they told me. And, although I had to do was tell them; them is what you need. I just lost my zest for sales. It became boring and just an obligation to pay bills. So, I really didn't want to go that route again. But I thanked him and told him I was still looking for another job. But, wow, the fact that he saw the best in me despite what everyone else saw. It made me feel optimistic that this may be a short-term thing.

He said he would investigate the charges, and because I thought he filed the charges, there may be a way to reduce them or get rid of them altogether. I waited a few days and talked to him, and he said that the state took it up because I had a knife. I explained the reasoning behind the knife, and he replied that it would be up to them.

I often wondered if I had taken the job would the charges have been reduced, but with all the other things that were occurring in my life, it seemed in line with everything this woman was doing to me. So, I had little faith that he could do anything to help me. But the mustard seed faith I did have, I believed that I would get out of this mess quickly once I explained to a judge what had happened. What judge would believe the woman was justified in damaging our home and

154

even threatening my father and other women. If anything, he would file charges against her; after he heard what she had done to my father and me, the judge would throw it out. Therefore, I wanted to get this over with quickly and without any major problems.

Chapter Fourteen

WILEY RIFF

I was home fresh out of jail and still very upset with my dad but was comforted in the fact that he came and bonded me out of that miserable place. I couldn't believe that the detective

I could not help but think my dad was the reason behind all this happening, and if he had not made the call, I would not be in so much trouble in the first place. But then I thought of the spell that was cast on my dad and fought myself to say he is not responsible. I didn't know what was coming my way with the new charges, and now, I could care less because the charges were nothing compared to the damage this woman had brought into my life. This woman was determined to get rid of me at every cost, and I was playing right into her hand. I could not remember what happened that day, and I also couldn't defend myself because I couldn't remember. My dad seemed to be ok and wasn't scared of me but instead seemed to be comforting me. I am not sure if it was out of guilt or he was indeed scared of me and was trying to play it off. He started to talk about the renovation again, and I said, "I will think about it. I really need to find a job."

Since the charges were against both my dad and Sidechick, I could not be around her at any time. I absolutely was overjoyed about that part of the charges because she could not come back into the house or around me. But then I remembered she had three days to put something in the house that could harm me. I had washed the walls down with pine sol and could not smell the horrible musty musk smell anymore and gave up trying to get my dad to smell it. I realized I was on my own and had to find someone else to help me since Michelle could no longer reach me. I found it strange that she suddenly disappeared as if she had fallen off the face of the earth. But as I thought more and more, I could just add it to the pile of things that made no sense or had no reasoning behind it.

I began applying for jobs online to take my mind off things and came across a job that was a shoe end for me; it was customer service, and cellular service all rolled up into one. I applied for the job and received an interview the next day. While I was filling out my pre-interview information, I received a call from a dear cousin named Pokey. She called because she had seen my mugshot in the local newspaper, and she knew something was wrong with me. Her first question was, "Cuz are you alright?" I began to explain to her what was going on.

She then said, "I looked at this picture of you and couldn't believe it because I've never seen you look this way in life."

I knew something was wrong. She told me Dad was wrong for calling the police, and he should have just backed out of the yard.

She also said, "She had heard things about this woman, and he is not the first one she has done this to."

When she said that to me, it made me think about more things that had happened. I remember, a man named Wylie Riff that always used to ride by our house and slowly watch our house. He had been doing this for a few years, and every time he would pass by, and I was there with my dad, my dad would say,

"There he goes again, I guess he's going to report back to Sidechick that he has seen another woman in my yard."

When I asked who this man was the first time, my dad said, "He was Sidechick's ex, and he watches him for her?"

I was so confused at what he said. He then said, "Remember when she came up in that new car when we first started talking? He is the one who bought her the car so she wouldn't have to depend on me."

Standing in disbelief, I just shook my head and said, "And, you know he bought her a car that sat in your yard."

He said, laughing, "Well, at least I don't have to buy her one."

I am sorry, I didn't see the humor. Because now this woman is still seeing and taking care of her husband and has a man who bought her a car and monitored her current boyfriend to report back to her. I couldn't make sense out of any of it, and neither could my dad. But he accepted it, and that was the problem. He accepted it, and she was free to do whatever she wanted to do but, he wasn't allowed to talk to anyone.

As the man continued to ride by our house, I would stare him down and wonder if he was rooted up too? I was told Sidechick caused him and his wife to divorce, and then she left

159

him. If this was the case, why was he still so interested in her life. Another fact that made no sense to me mentally but, in a different world, the spiritual world, it made perfect sense because this man was doing things that made him look desperate and a stalker, and every time he would come by our house, my dad would get a call from Sidechick asking him who was at our house?

Sidechick eventually gave the car back to him and told my dad she gave it back because he bought it for her to only be able to meet him. Wylie Riff was dating my dad's cousin as well Arbri, and she was aware of the affair with Sidechick. She also knew he was still coming by our house because dad let her know. Arbri, was also very sick and didn't follow it up but, she knew, and when she confronted Wylie, he cursed her out and dragged my dad's name through the mud to her, and she ended up believing everything he said.

My dad says, "If she wants to be a fool, so be it. I just want him to leave me alone. If he wants Sidechick, he can have her and take away all this bullshit I go through."

Once again, I tried to tell my dad; you could get out of this if you really wanted to get out of it.

Dad said, "How, how can I get out of this without getting hurt or Ma getting hurt or you?"

When my dad said that to me, I stopped him mid-sentence and said, "Wait, what did you say?"

He stopped as if he had said something wrong. I said, "Dad, what did you say about us getting hurt?"

He said, "Sidechick said, if I leave her for Ma or anyone, she is going to kill them and me."

I said, "What, daddy? And you are still with this woman, and you know she is crazy and means it once again."

But what do I have to do with this, and why is she trying to hurt me? He said, "Because she feels you don't like her, and you are for Ma. And she doesn't like the inference in her business."

I said, "Dad, you are my business, and any woman who threatens your safety and well-being, or any of your family members doesn't love you. Dad, I want you to stay away from this woman."

He then proceeds to talk about how her family is very dangerous, how all her kids carry guns, and how they will hurt us if I hurt their mom. I told my dad, I'm not afraid of any of her children or her, and it seems that you are making any and every excuse under the sun to leave this low-life tramp alone. I am

161

going to get to the bottom of this mess, and when I do, she is going to wish she never met me.

Dad said, "Jen, you don't want to mess with them. They have killed people and got away with it."

I looked at my dad and said, "Really, dad, and you know this, and you still want to be a part of it? I don't believe any of the war stories you are coming up with because it's all coming from a woman that would lie on her own child to get a man. So, please just stop."

But my dad insisted. "Just let me handle it."

I knew once again we were not safe. I called Xfinity and scheduled an alarm system to be installed to show every corner of the house from front to back but, how could I protect the house inside, especially if I was not there. There was no way I could guarantee dad would resist this woman if she wanted to come into the house.

I decided since the back area had a door that sealed us off from the main house, the best thing to do was change the locks. I started working on all of this to keep us secured when dad told me she was threatening him, ma, and me. I was again distraught and confused but wanted to do everything possible to keep Lagearld and me safe. This was no way to live, and I knew I would not be able to maintain it for a long period of time. But I needed to make sure my dad was healthy.

Dad's appointment for his prostate was scheduled for the following day, and I intended to go to the doctor with him since this was the primary reason I moved home. I got up and got dressed, only for my dad to call me upstairs and tell me he preferred if I didn't go to the appointment because Sidechick was going to be there. I became upset at even the sound of her name and asked why? I began to explain how I moved home for this very reason, and there is no reason she should get to go, and I do not go to your doctor's appointments. I am your daughter, and she is no one. He told me it was already planned, and he didn't want to argue with her.

I said, "Well, what about me?"

I am not going to let this woman go to my dad's appointment, and that's what I am here for. I also am not going to let her dictate when and where I can go concerning you. I am going, and that's that. Dad gave me the address of the doctor's office and shook his head as he went out the door to pick up Sidechick, although what I had just said to him. He knew I wasn't supposed to be around this lady yet; he still listened to her and fought me about going to the doctor.

163

At, this point, I got mad at anything he said and did not care how disrespectful I was because I felt he put me in this situation. I was so angry still and wondered whether he ever thought about how I was feeling and the fact that he kept on betraying me and only thinking about Sidechick's feelings and not mine.

As, I drove down the highway to the doctor's office, I called my mommy to tell her what was going on.

She said, "Does your father know that you have changed your entire life and moved home to help him because he is sick?"

I said, "Yes, and he still is putting this woman before me. Now, he is trying to stop me from going to the doctor's appointment."

Mommy said, "He knows you are not supposed to be around this woman, so why is he doing this?"

I said, "Mommy, please tell me this woman has something strong on our dad to make him turn against us, and he knows this ain't right."

I have never seen someone who sees that his child is there for him but would rather have a woman come in between him and you to get what she wants. It is not right! But you go on to the doctor's office and stand by your dad. No matter what she says or does, you continue to stand by him, and this will all be over soon with the help of God.

I got to the doctor's office and went to the address my dad gave me, and as I walked into the office, I saw Sidechick sitting in the waiting area but did not see my dad. I thought he was in the bathroom, and since I could not be in the same area with her, I waited in the hallway for him to come out of the bathroom. He came out of the opposite door, and I said, "Dad, where are you coming from?"

He said he was in with the doctor. I looked at him and said, "You were in with the doctor? I was supposed to go in with you to find out what is going on."

He kind of brushed it off and said, "If you want to go in to talk to the doctor, go right in that door right there," while walking away from me as if I was annoying him.

He then went to the waiting room and said, "Sidechick, let's go," and started walking out of the entrance door.

I said, "Dad, what is going on?"

He said, "They want to do a procedure on me where they will put a scope down my penis to look at my prostate. I didn't tell you this but, I have been bleeding since 2013."

I said, "Bleeding? Are you serious, dad?"

He said, "Yes, I have, and I thought it had stopped because I no longer saw any blood in my underwear or when I peed, but the doctor just did a urine test, and the blood is still there."

Of course, I went there and said, so you have been seeing this woman since 2013 and have been bleeding and didn't want to know what was causing it? And she loves you so much but didn't even suggest that you go to a doctor to see what is going on? Thank God I came home because, if not, you would be dead.

Once, again as he walked to his truck, he said, "Jennifer, let me handle it."

I was so tired of hearing him say that to me. It was always either "it didn't matter" or "let me handle it." Everything mattered, and he wasn't handling a damn thing, and I was tired of it. I came back home just as mad as I left and prepared for my interview that afternoon. I received a call around 3 pm, and after the interview, I was told I needed to do an in-person interview at the site location the following day. I was so excited because at least I would be out of the house and occupy myself not to have to deal with my dad and this situation.

I literally loathed the idea of talking to him. I felt the anger I had in me was very justified, and I wasn't going to let it go, especially not now because of the doctor's visit that day. I had to fight a woman who wanted control just to go to my dad's doctor's visit, and she wasn't even his wife. What next? I have often heard be careful about what you ask for because you just might get it.

After the interview, I was offered a job as a Call center representative for Verizon, 15.00 an hour, But the interviewer felt I was overqualified for this position due to my work history and background. The interviewer said I was strong enough to be in the management program and placed me in the management program at the same job. I would receive a salary pay vs. an hourly pay, And, although that was more in line with my work portfolio, I wanted to take the first job offer to get me back to work and keep me out of the line of fire with my dad and Sidechick. I went and took my drug test, signed consent for my background check, and waited for the call to start work.

During the time I was waiting to start work, I grew tired of my dad asking me what about the renovation? I really did not want to do anything else concerning the renovation because we were in the whole negative $10.000 and the way my dad turned on me when I told him to get our money back within the first week. He did not listen; I was very skeptical about doing anything else concerning our house.

I finally decided to find someone to fix the kitchen floor, add the double car garage, and give me the gable porch I wanted for my alone time. I contacted Angie's list on the internet, which seemed like a reputable referral company, to find someone who could build the garage and porch and fix the subflooring work in the kitchen. The garage and porch were additions. Therefore, it would be a new addition to the house. But the kitchen was different; I felt because it was double the work that had already been done.

There was absolutely no reason there should be a hump on the kitchen floor, but as I said, because my dad was so easygoing, people just felt they could run over him, and he let them. The kitchen floor needed to be removed, and new wood needed to be installed. After a few people called back, I turned them down because of the price. A guy named Augustus called me and said, I can come up tomorrow and price all you want to do. I was so excited and said OK, thanks, we will see you then.

When Augustus called and told me he would be late coming up due to another job, I automatically thought, here we go again for a repeat of what we had already been through with Eduardo.

I was still second-guessing myself. Therefore, I spent a lot of time reaching out to everyone, asking them am I right about something or should I do it another way. It became to the point I could not make decisions alone. I accompanied this by also listening to my dad and becoming more and more angrier as I talked to him, asking me a thousand questions for something he could do himself. Oh, and did I say that dad had not slept in his bed since the night I got out of jail. Every day I would listen to them argue about what he was doing and who was over at his house and when he was coming to her house and after the argument carried on for the entire day. I watched my dad go out the door to stay in the projects. This gave me an added thing every time to bring up to him when we argued because he couldn't give me a reason why.

I was arrested on December 10, 2018, and I got out of jail on December 13, 2018. We hired Augustus in February of 2019, therefore for the last two months, my dad was still dealing with this troll and still going to her house every night afterward, and I could not stand it. It seemed like he dug a knife deeper in my back each night that he left me. The betrayal was too much to take that I made it my mission to say something to him about it each night. I could not understand how he could still be with someone who brought all these charges against his daughter. Now, at the time, I still didn't know what dad had said to the officers, and I didn't care. I cared about my feelings and how this man was betraying me at every corner and every turn. Each day they argued. Each day we argued, and each night he went out of the door to live yet another night in the projects.

When we hired Augustus, he gave us a quote of $13,000 for labor to build the porch and the garage. My dad always felt that buying the materials and paying for the labor was the right way to go. But I wasn't so sure since we had already lost the 10,000. But I listened to him because it was his money, and if he made the decision, I would not be blamed again for any problems encountered with this renovation. Augustus required a down payment of $2300 to get started, and I said Dad, another red flag, we should not pay him upfront. We just went through this with Eduardo, and I'm telling you I don't feel good about this at all. Dad gave me every excuse in the book why we should pay this money upfront, and I was against each of them.

He said, "Well, you handle it. I put you in charge, and you make the decision."

When Augustus came to pick up the deposit, I told him I wanted to talk to him, and I explained why we did not feel comfortable giving money upfront, and I would like to see some of the work done before we give any money. Augustus spoke of how he had to pay the helpers, and he had to secure the money to make sure he was covered on the money he would be losing by taking this job. Before I could say anything, Dad interrupted me and said, Sir, we will pay you the down payment. I turned around like the girl on the exorcist and said, "Dad!"

I said, "Sir give us a moment and let me talk to my dad alone."

We went out to the backyard, and I said, "Dad, I thought we said it was not a good idea to work with this guy if we don't see the work upfront. You know what we just went through with Eduardo, and I thought you were going to let me handle it. So why did you tell this man we would pay him when I was only doing what we agreed on yesterday?"

Dad said, "Jennifer (anytime he was mad or wanted to make me mad, he called me Jennifer), we can't hold up this man from losing work, and he must pay his helpers so, just give him the money."

I rolled my eyes so hard at my dad. I had this man where he would show us the work before getting the money.

171

I said, "You give him the money, dad; you are not going to blame me when he does the same thing to you that Eduardo did to you," and I walked off and went to my room.

Chapter Fifteen

The Renovation continues, A contractor Nightmare

Dad called me to say Augustus was supposed to start the following day at 11 am. He said that he would not be off work by then and asked if I would stand in for him. I did not want to because I was too angry to even speak to him. Again, simply because my dad had divided yet once again in front of the help. Also, because I knew where this would go, I would be the problem, and my dad would play the nice guy, and he could get away with anything he wanted to do.

I read Augustus just like I read Eduardo when he did not show up on the first day until 4 pm. I went to dad and said, "This is going to be a big problem."

Dad made excuses for him, "Jennifer, he has other customers."

"That is the same thing you said about Eduardo, and he has $10,000 of your money."

Augustus had written down the materials and given them to dad, and he went and got them. When my dad came into the yard, I looked at the truck and said, "Dad, why are you going to get the materials if you are paying for them, and he is doing the labor?"

He said, "I told him I would help him out since he was coming from another job."

I lost it. "Dad, why are you helping someone who has a crew? Where are they? And why can't he go and pick up the materials if we have already paid for them?"

He told me to let it go and let him do what he wanted. And, once again, I did and went back to my room.

The second day and every day after that for about two weeks Augustus, told him he would be there by 1 pm and showed up at 3 or 4 and even seven sometimes. He would leave our floor in the kitchen and now the dining room because it was diagnosed to have rotten wood as well. It was completely open, and anything, including spiders and snakes or rats or any small animal or reptile, could have crept into our house. And, every day, he would show up, and dad would say, "Oh, it's alright."

174

He would sit with him alone, and he would do the work. I would come in and ask Augustus a lot of questions as to why the floors were still not completed and when he was going to start on the porch and the garage and would get excuse after excuse of how he had to go to the hospital with his brother, or he got here too late to get any work done. I would get angrier and angrier every day because he would not clean up and wood and dust and turmoil were in the front entrance of the house and the kitchen.

I repeatedly asked that he clean up his mess and close the floor, and he kept talking to my dad about it taking time. And, when I finally confronted him and told him that we needed to change the contract because the floors were taking too long, Dad stepped in yet again and said, "No, he is doing fine."

I hollered so much that day and told them both off. I could not believe that my dad accepted all of this and let this man run all over him. When I discussed changing the contract and Augustus agreed because he no longer wished to work with me because I always was fussing and cussing him out because he wouldn't do what he was paid for, I decided again to step out of the renovation.

175

On the following day, he showed up yet again around 4 pm and hesitantly gave me a new contract. When I looked at the contract, and saw a difference in the amount owed to Augustus.

I said, "These amounts weren't right. Why is your amount lesser than the original contract?"

He said, "Ahh, that's because your dad gave me $2000 the other day to pay my workers." I said, "Firstly, where are your workers? because since you started two weeks ago, I have not seen one."

He said, "I have workers working for me on other jobs."

"Dad, why did you give him $2000.00, and you haven't seen one worker, and the floor is still open, my porch or your garage have not even been started yet, and you're giving money behind my back! What are you doing?"

I spared no feelings and no expense to tell my dad in front of Augustus that he was wrong. I am here trying to renovate a house for him, and he keeps giving the money away. I had enough. We were in a fix and had a lot of things moving around us. Why would you give Augustus anything, and you are sitting there with him every day and see him not finishing the work.

I then saw Augustus cut off a piece of rotten wood and attach new wood to the old wood. I said, "What are you doing? We have new wood for the floors."

He tried to explain to me that all the wood did not need to be used, and he would cut out what was needed and attach new wood to existing wood that was ok. I disagreed with him and asked what was the need for it when we had already bought new wood and that is what should be used. I then went back to the money.

"Please do not ask my father for any more money behind my back, and there will not be a need to ask him because I am taking the porch and the garage from you since you can't even get the floor done."

My dad tried to step in, and I said, "Nope, not this time dad."

This man is a con artist, and now you have given him the money he did not deserve, and we are not going to lose one more dime. I walked out, and as I walked away, Augustus asked my father, "Is she paying for any of this?"

I turned around and told him, "No, I'm not paying a dime, which is why you deal with my father and not me. Because I know you are no good and can't do what you agreed to, and if

177

this floor isn't finished by Friday, I'm going to be the one who sues your ass."

I have had enough; we were not safe in our home due to the floor being taken up. We couldn't use the sink; therefore, I must wash the dishes in the tub in the bathroom. Not my dad; he had a sink upstairs, and this was not right. He told me this might take two weeks tops and, we are not even done with the kitchen. I made it clear that I would find someone else to do the work and build the garage and the porch. Dad, said nothing because he knew I was right and acted like a little child when I scolded him about giving the money to Augustus. We argued in between the Sidechick calling, and I told him this was it.

"If you are going to continue giving away the money you need to handle the renovation. I am tired of you betraying me and sabotaging me."

I really wanted to know why my dad repeatedly changed in front of the contractors and always was against me. I made perfect sense yet, he ignored me and did the complete opposite every time. I also wanted to understand why every time it happened, I got so angry with my dad that I blew a gasket every day, so it seemed. It felt like my arrest day repeatedly. I was always angry, and I would lose it because he wouldn't listen to me.

If he only would listen to me and do what we agreed to do when he was in front of the contractor, we wouldn't have a problem. But he changed on me every time. But that wasn't the bad part. After every interaction with Augustus saying, "Get the job done, or why didn't you come to work today?" My dad would come to me and apologize for going against me. When I would bring up the things he said and did, he acted as if he did not remember what he had said to the contractor and tried to insist I wasn't right on my assessment but apologized for doing what I was accusing him of.

My dad's mental space had slowed down tremendously, and he didn't remember a lot of things. I didn't know whether to attribute it to the fact that he was 70 years old or someone deliberately was dumbing him down to the point where he could remember nothing from one minute to another.

He was like an empty shell with limited capabilities when it came to handling business or dealing with people. If it did not come in an envelope, he would be lost and couldn't get anything done, which puzzled me because my father was always sharp as a tack in anything. I mean, how else could he win so much

179

money gambling to build our home if he didn't know how to work numbers or know when someone was trying to beat him. But, in this house and any conversation, we had he would never be able to comprehend what I was saying, and if he messed up, he apologized, and although that may not seem strange to some, to me it wasn't the way, I have lived my life for 48 years.

I learned from my father, which is why I couldn't accept the things that he was doing as normal. At this point, I couldn't say I didn't know what was going on. I had confirmations every day, and every conversation I had with him to support something was being made to him to dumb him down this way. If Sidechick could dumb him down, then she could control him. Because that was all this was about. But what did she really want? Did she want him, the house, the cars, the assets? What was her end game? I kept trying to find reasoning for it, and nothing made sense. She had no stakes in the house or said so because something happened to cause my dad to keep her out of the house business. I assumed it was because he got mad about the furniture and banned her from any house business. But, if he let her come back in the house, wouldn't that decision just have gone away when he allowed her to come back in the house. But it did not, and I was even more confused.

Finally, Augustus said he was coming to finish the floor after I gave him a hard deadline to have it fixed by that Friday or else. And he called my dad and told him he was in Las Vegas with his brother's because he was sick. I didn't believe that any more than he was late every day because he had another job to do. This man was just as shady as Eduardo, and the weirdest thing about it was, he said the same things as Eduardo. He would call my dad instead of calling me, which further confused the situation and caused even more of a rift between me and my father. He told my dad he would be back the following Wednesday and never showed up. The house had been open for about three weeks, and the job was still not done. I told dad I would send a demand letter and give him to have the job done by Friday of that week, and if it was not done and the floor was not sealed, I was going to file charges in Magistrate court him as well. Dad finally agreed and told him he needed to come to finish the job.

He came the following days on time and completed the flooring work with no more excuses. But why did it take that to get the work complete? Because he wanted to work with dad and not me, that made all the difference. Two weeks later, our kitchen floor fell, and I called Augustus and told him if he did not come and take the floor back up and repair the entire floor, I would sue him for the money we paid him, and because my dad had gone behind my back, we were out of an additional $4300.00. Augustus agreed to come back and fix the floor and took the floor back up again for a second time and began to work and I let him know there would be no more old wood to new wood because the floor had fallen, and apparently that did not work. He got angry and started pacing back and forth, I guess having a come to Jesus meeting with me, and I could care less about him trying to do the best he could, and all I did was fuss and argue and give him a hard time.

I told Augustus, "Sorry, that doesn't work for me. You have been now paid $4300.00, and the floor has fallen, and you are responsible and bound by the contract."

I also explained the contract would be amended yet again to show the new repairs that were needed for him to fulfill his obligation. After he spent about 15 minutes pacing and spilling his guts, trying to deflect blame as to why he didn't want to work with me anymore, I gave him the answer we were both comfortable with as I grew tired of this foolishness.

I gave him a deadline of 3 days to have the floor complete, and if it were not complete, I would sue him for the work he botched and get our money back. And I wasn't accepting any excuse. Dad stepped in for the last time and told him to take his time, and he looked over at me and laughed in my face. But this I was ready and gave Augustus a final demand letter dated for that day and told him and my father, if the floor is not done in 3 days, I'm going to sue. I wasn't playing any more games with any contractors or my dad. Augustus came up the following day at 4 pm and worked for 3 hours to fix where the floor had fallen and never returned. I went to the magistrate yet again and filed paperwork on Augustus for faulty work and sued him for $4300.00, and now we were out of $14300.00 and had a floor that was still open and unsteady.

I literally screamed as I got back in the car from filing the paperwork. When I came home from the courthouse, Augustus was in the yard and wanted to complete the work. I said, "I would advise you to get the tools that you have laid around our kitchen and dining room for three weeks and meet me in court. I will find someone else to complete the work."

Dad said, "When this is over with, I'm going to tell you a few things."

I said, "I would advise you to tell me now, because the way things are going, we will not have enough money to build the

183

garage and porch. We have lost so much money, not including the materials that we have purchased. We are almost out of money. So, whatever you tell me, it better be that all this is your fault because you didn't listen."

"It was because you chose to fight me in front of them, and all they both were doing was playing you. I have been right about both the people, and you refused to listen to me, and now what are we going to do," I added.

Dad suggested that we call back to Merrill lynch and see if we could borrow more money to replace the money we had lost while waiting to go to court for now. And guess who would have to prove both cases to the judge? Me! Make it make sense. I couldn't and grew a huge disdain for my dad for repeatedly creating this situation, and it did not have to happen that way. Now, I had to fight to get back the money I was against giving to them both, and I was very angry at both because they both were the same jack leggers who conned people out of their hard-earned money and gave subpar work and terrible work ethics because people like my dad allowed them to. My dad trusted them and didn't trust me, and that is what I summed it up to be. We were able to get an additional $21,000 from the 401k to cover the deficit, and that helped because we still had the porch, the garage, the cabinets, the flooring, the windows, and the roof to be installed. I had about $8000.00 left from the previous amount requested, so I had to make a miracle happen. There was no way I could do it by buying materials. Therefore, we applied for a Home Depot card to handle the materials.

Now, I had to find someone to fix the flooring due to the still dipping in certain areas. I found a guy named Kurt, and he did subflooring work. Kurt was a family man and a very religious guy. He was real easygoing and had his son working with him because he had no one who wanted to work. Bobby was a great kid but, it seemed like he didn't want to be there. I could just tell it in his demeanor and often tried to talk to him to make him smile but, he didn't want to work. Kurt came in and took up the subflooring for the entire kitchen and determined that the job was a shimmy sham job, and by Augustus putting old wood to new wood, it created a domino effect, and that's why the floor fell.

He said, "The entire floor would be better off being scrapped and new wood to replace it all in order not to have any more dips or the floor waving."

He gave us a price of $2300.00.

I said, "So you mean to tell me we are going to have to pay for the floor twice."

He said, "Yes, ma'am."

He didn't know what he was doing, and now the wood was uneven, and it would just be easier to start from scratch. I just shook my head at my dad and called the planning board and updated the permit to reflect Kurt's name as the new contractor. I then signed another contract with Kurt and explained there would not be any money up front. We have gone through much, and I am not willing to lose any more money. I called Aces Hardware since it was in Thomson and ordered the materials. Kurt came the following day and built the entire kitchen floor in 3 hours. What was Augustus doing that? It took six weeks for something that could be done in 3 hours. Absolutely nothing beneficial to us but, he would be dealt with along with Eduardo on another day.

Kurt did such a great job. I asked if he did any builder work? He said yes, and I gave him the measurements for the garage and porch. He gave us a price, and it seemed reasonable, and we planned to get started by ordering the trusses for the garage.

The porch had to be extended because the porch was long but not big enough to support the porch I wanted; therefore, I had to find someone who poured the concrete. I contacted a man by the name of Mike who gave me a joint price for pouring both. Mike came and measured the porch and the garage and began to pour the concrete that Eduardo should have completed, and even gave me a stoop and back porch for the garage. I really thought my trouble was over, and maybe just maybe, I could get this remodel done without any more problems. After the concrete was poured, a few days later, the floor cracked.

Mike said, "All floors crack, but he didn't understand why this one did because he made cuts in it and no cars had been on it yet."

He just didn't understand how this could happen. The porch had had an issue, too, because the step was too small to support the porch. I spoke to Mike, and he got angry because I asked for a discount on the garage price due to the crack, and I asked for the porch step to be extended. When I asked for the discount, dad said, "Why Jennifer? Maybe, this is the best that he can do?"

I said, "Dad, so you are going to do this again? Let me speak to you in the house."

"Dad, who is in charge again?"

He said, "Jennifer, I know what I said but, you are being nasty to him, and this man does not have to honor any of your requests."

I said, "Yes, he does. That is the purpose of the contract. And just because we are in the hole, that doesn't mean we have to accept what someone throws at us."

But why did the floor crack? That was what we really needed to find out? Let him fix it if he is willing to fix the porch step. We will ask for a discount on the garage floor since no car has been on it and no explanation as to why it cracked. We came back outside, and Mike agreed to discount the garage an additional $500 to cover the crack. He widened the step to make it match the porch, and he fixed the concrete that looked as though it was cracking on the sides of the porch.

When it was all done, it was beautiful; I got Bert, a friend, to paint the porch white to match the trim of the house. Next was the walls. They were going to be made from cement blocks to support the rest of the house. Because my dad used cement blocks, the house was very sturdy, and I didn't see a need to change anything. Because as we saw, the floor in the dining room and kitchen were both made from wood and because of that we had to replace the floor three times. I just didn't want to

188

risk it. I hired a person from Keysville, GA, to whom Kurt referred me. Nate brought a crew of guys to lay the blocks, which turned into a nightmare. The garage was a custom job because my dad wanted the diameter to match the other side of the house, which was a 24 by 44.

When I spoke with the guy Nate who was laying the blocks, I explained to him that I didn't have a contractor but knew what I wanted. When he finished the blocks, the back door wasn't the correct size and Kurt, complained because he gave him the right measurements. This created a major problem for so many reasons. During the time the crew was working, I saw his workers continuously going back and forth to the truck they were in, and as they came back, I overheard one of them saying, "If I don't have my beer, I can't work right!"

I went to Nate and said, "So you have employees out here drinking? No wonder my door is off."

He got upset and argued with me as if I was wrong. I paid him, and he left. At this point, I was tired of arguing with every person I hired and again began to question my ability to do this renovation. It just seemed like there was something wrong every time or something unexplainable happening to cause problems.

189

There was never any peace or a job that was done correctly, and no matter what, it always ended up in an argument.

On the day, Nate and his crew were laying the bricks. Wylie Riff came by the house and completely stopped in front of my dad's house, and told my dad to stay away from Sidechick. I went outside behind my dad and asked this man if he was crazy?

He said, "She's been telling me what you are saying about me, and I want you to stay away from her."

My dad told him if he came back to his property again, he would kill him, and he was trying to hear nothing that he was saying to him. Dad waved his hand at him as if he wasn't listening to what he was saying anymore.

Wylie said, "I got you, I got you, and drove off."

Then the Sidechick called, and my dad preceded to tell him about the visit. She said, "I don't know why he did that but, what are you doing? Where are you at? Who is over there? What are you doing, Bobby?"

My dad cursed her out that day and told her to leave him the hell alone. She called back eight times in a row, and they continued to argue. She asked what time he was coming over to her house, and he told her he may not.

She began to threaten him and said, "If you don't, I already have told you what I'm going to do."

I asked Dad what she meant; he said, "Don't worry about it, just let me handle it."

I had an uneasy feeling about this situation and felt that my dad would stay at home that night because this man threatened him. But, after Nate and his crew finished the block laying, my dad made his usual exit out the door and went to her house and spent the night with a woman who just threatened him once again. I felt Betrayed once again, with chaos and pure hell going on in our home, and now my father was being threatened.

Our situation was getting more critical by the day. My dad seemed like he didn't have any fight in him left, almost as if he was afraid of Sidechick. No matter what she did to him, he took it and tried to sweep it under the rug. We continued, and the building inspector came out and said the front of the garage was not right and a support beam would have to be placed over the garage. Kurt came and measured and ordered the beam. He was very upset because Nate did not lay the blocks the correct way, which created the need for the beam. And he called and told him but, there was nothing Nate was willing to do to fix it.

Kurt finally got the beam correctly in place after it took about five days to make because it was a special order. Once he installed the beam, we were ready for the woodwork, including the trusses to be done and then sheetrock to be laid in the garage. Kurt nailed in the trusses, and the garage was near completion. We were going like clockwork, and the sheetrock installer Woody came and laid the sheetrock for the walls and ceiling. A couple of days later, the ceiling split down the middle. Once again, there was no reason this should have happened, but he stated to him it seemed as if the garage had shifted. Kurt checked and saw no shift but, more work had to be done to fix the now cracked ceiling. The inspector returned and said a crawl space needed to be in the garage just in case we needed to repair anything at the top of the house. Woody put a crawl space in the ceiling while he was repairing the sheet rock, and the garage was complete. The electrician was already involved and had a problem with running the wiring for the garage and the porch but maneuvered through and got his work done.

The garage doors had to be ordered, but they had to be reordered due to the issues with the beam having to be placed in the garage. Kurt became very frustrated at all of the things that were happening and said, "He was tired of all the problems, and it was delaying him from other jobs."

He then began to work on another job and left our job incomplete and until all the issues were completed. I got upset because I felt that he should have stayed and could be doing other things, and he told me he had been on this job too long, and after going back and forth for a day or so, he told me to find someone else to finish the job. I said, "But we still owe you $1200.00."

He said, "There is just too much confusion and problems and rework, and I need to make money. I am losing back; just keep the money; there is something going on with this house. This is not normal, and I just don't want to finish the job."

The one person who was doing the job correctly and left us with money on the books being owed to him. Nothing made any sense, and finally, I had enough. I left for Atlanta the next day to find some help to help me to get rid of the turmoil that plagued us. Dad and I didn't argue with each other or Kurt for the first time, but we got the same outcome. I went to Atlanta and went back to Michelle's office with the hope that she may have come back to work. Her sign was still up on the billboard; therefore, it gave me hope. But, when I got to the door, the building was empty, and I just dropped my head. I began to search on the internet for spiritual healers and came across a lady's name, and by that name, I felt she could help me. She was a spiritual woman who specialized in removing spells and roots. I did not have any guidelines to go by or didn't know what to ask her so, I told her what Michelle had told me, and I needed help. The woman then told me her fee and told me to come to her house. I went to her house started off by reading my palm and telling me the same things that Michelle told me. She referenced Buck Buck, and when she asked about my back, I knew she was speaking the truth. She then told me what this woman was trying to do to my dad and that this woman was not working alone. She, too, described the woman to me, and I knew once again it was the Sidechick. She described her hair changing and said she was very controlling, and I had to work quickly to remove it before it grew back. I said, why would it grow back?

She said, "If the spell is not reversed, it could come back with a vengeance even though I had the snakelike cyst removed. If it is not removed and certain spell breakers are not performed to kill it, it will grow back like a tree root."

I was ready to do what she wanted me to do, and then she told me it would cost me $3500.00 because of the seriousness of

194

the spell. She said, "This woman sent whatever she had of yours and your father to Jamaica."

And without me knowing what spell it was, I would have to try several things. I felt doomed because I did not have $3500.00. I had access to the money for the renovation, but things were so tight that I couldn't do it. Also, in speaking to my friend Julia, she stated to me I should not have to pay a dime to have anything removed, and God would remove it for free. I then left the woman's house and headed home with a lot to think about concerning the removal of this spell.

As I drove back home, I tried to convince myself that I often said I could replace the money because I was waiting on my unemployment to start but didn't want to take the chance of not replacing the money. I went back home, and when I got home, I had received a message from the company I was supposed to start at for the sales position. I returned the call, and I asked when my start date was; and the Hiring Manager apologized first and then told me that my background had come back and unfortunately, I could not start due to pending charges on my record. I asked her to hold on, muted the phone, and began to scream. I was livid and felt that after waiting nearly three weeks to hear back from them was unacceptable and furthermore, for them to tell me that the pending charges are still considered a reason not to hire because they could not predict the outcome of the case and did not want to hire me and might lose me if I am convicted.

I felt whatever happened to innocent before proven guilty. This seemed to me to contradict that saying, and I needed a job. When the hiring manager told me this, I tried to remain as calm as possible and asked her could I speak to someone in upper management. She then began explaining the policies and referred me back to the new hire paperwork I had signed. I had no response or recourse. The consequences of my actions finally hit me, and she told me that until these charges were adjudicated, I would have the same problem with all major employers. I got off the phone with her and went to my dad's room and told him what she had told me. As I walked into the room, the horrible musty musk smell was all over the room. I stopped midstride and stood in the middle of the floor. There was no way I was getting any of it on me. I told him so now; I can't even get a job in my field because of this mess.

He said, "I tried to stop you, you wouldn't listen. I felt like I had to get out of there because one, I felt dizzy, and two, I was going to fuss and fight with him again, and I was tired and just done."

I could not get this man to see that he played a big part in this by bringing that woman to our home, but also even staying with her after she damaged our furniture. But, what she did to me was unbelievable and unforgivable because he continued to see her and further caused the pain I was feeling. There was no way I could not curse my father out, so I left and called the people closest to me and vented to them.

I thank God for them because I would not have made it without them. A lot of times, they didn't know when I was talking to them that they were making my decisions for me because I couldn't. Every decision I made on my own, I had problems because my balance was mentally off, which caused me to make decisions that could hurt me. This was a terrible state to be in, and combined with trying to tell people what was being done to me and not being believed, I almost completely lost it at times. I thought hard about borrowing the money from my dad but, I couldn't bring myself to do that to him, I never steal from anyone, and my dad was no different. But, at this point. I never steal from anyone, and my dad was no different.

But, at this point, I became desperate to get help to fix this problem once and for all, and I knew dad wasn't going to give it to me, so I had to go out and get it myself, and that's what I started to do.

Chapter Sixteen

Time to go

I had no one to listen to me to make my dad see what was being done both to him and me. My dad became so distant from me. We never talked like we did before. He would consistently accuse me of things that I had no idea of what he was talking about most times. I could not get him to see I was his daughter and not his enemy. After I got out of jail and tried to adapt to my new normal life, I tried to stay away from my dad deliberately and not go near him because of the constant smell of the horrible musty musk. When I would be around him, I could not have much time alone to try and reel him back in because the phone would ring, and he would start arguing, and it wouldn't let up until his normal exit out of the house. Therefore, I tried to keep my sanity and wanted nothing to do with him or this woman.

As I stated before, I was in an altered state and mentally imbalanced with no end in sight and no one to help me in the spiritual realm. I couldn't get a job in my profession because the pending charges would hold me back if I applied. Therefore, I had to think of other ways to get income and secondary jobs. My first job was at Blimpy's, a corner store right down from my house. I needed something close since I was still in charge of my nephew's care. Since we had just moved, I was still waiting for the region of DBHDD to transfer the funding for his care. I was the person in charge of his budget and needed the funding to pay for someone to watch him within this area.

Another reason why I needed to work was I also was still paying for this shiny new red CTS Cadillac, and I didn't want to lose it. My dad always told me to "Buy a car to buy and not to trade." So, of course, I didn't want to lose it. His words during my upbringing/training meant something to me, so I tried to keep my car even without a job. I was determined, and it was a beautiful car with a fresh paint job and no blemishes. I had started talking to the owner of Blimpy's about a job since I had moved back home from Atlanta. I went in one day to buy some things, and he asked if I still needed a job. I hesitated because he only offered me $8.00 an hour. I had not made that since I was 18 years old. Since I started in the cellular world and Corporate America, I always made 20.000, starting in 1995 to about 65,000 a year, but now I had been reduced to a low-paying job and could do nothing about it. This was my new normal.

On the day I started the job, and found myself sweeping and mopping and running the side liquor store and cashiering. Every day, I worked I would see someone who recognized me and asked what I was doing there. One day, I was working in the liquor store, and this Jamaican guy came in, and instantly, I knew who he was. He was the husband of the bootlegger.

As He came into the store, I started unknowingly getting really nervous. He had multiple sales, and each one of them I gave him back incorrect change, and there were at least five transactions. It was almost as if he was annoying me to mess up my countback of money. I just felt uneasy because he knew who I was. I am sure. After he left, something said to go outside and look at my car. When I walked around it that was a long scratch on the back of my car on the rear ride side. I had just gotten my car washed, and I knew there were no scratches prior to coming to work. He was one of the first customers to come in when I got to work, so; it had to be him. From that moment, I started carrying a weapon in my car. A blade because I didn't know what these people were capable of, and if he was that bold to vandalize my car in broad daylight out of spite and evilness, what else would he or any of them do.

WhenI began working; I got inspired again concerning love. I started trying to make myself more noticeable, my hair was growing back, and I was trying to feel normal and sexy as I used to be and feel. There was this guy who lived in my neighborhood named Trouble, and for the last four years, all we did was remain friends. We spent time together when I came home but never really took him seriously. I was a cougar and preferred young men because, let's face it. It kept me young sexually. There was no other reason I enjoyed being a cougar. It always came with more stress than needed, and I always got disrespected; therefore, why was I a cougar, only for the sexual benefits.

On the first day home, I pulled around the corner, and he was standing on his porch. I hadn't seen him for about a year and was told he was with his daughter's mom. I was surprised and stopped and spoke and he told me to call him. We instantly hit it off as always but, this time was different. He was fresh out of prison and didn't have a car, so of course, I had to go get him. But I didn't mind because I was just thankful to have the company. At that point, any man paying attention to me and looking and me and finally noticing me was a plus, and my self-esteem was so low I didn't care. I was desperate for the attention of a man.

On the first night, we chilled and the entire week thereafter. Every night he would sleepover at my house but, still, we had no sex. I remember one day, dad came into the living room, and we were sitting watching a movie while I was greasing his hair, and dad looked with a sign of curiosity. Because unless it was my husband, I never brought anyone home. If I did, they were serious. And, we had only been talking for a couple of weeks. We continued to see each other the same routine, get up in the morning to take him home to go to work and pick him up after work the same to spend the night. And, then it happened we made love for the first time. It was the most breathtaking experience at first because he was so into me, and I was so unsure about myself, and I remember when he climbed on top of me. Suddenly there was a green light between us, and I looked through it, and his face was different. I said, "You look different."

He said, "So do you, what the fuck?"

And we stopped and stared at each other for a brief 20 seconds. He was a very light-skinned slender tall guy, but the guy I saw was dark-skinned, and he looked possessed. I started trying to get loose from him; when I realized it wasn't his face, the demonic spirit was holding me down. That is the only thing I can explain why trouble went from being another man inside of me and a different complexion match. This was a man but, it wasn't him. When I finally screamed, get off me and pushed him off me. Trouble and I sat on the same side of the bed, and he asked, "What just happened?"

I said, "I don't know but, that wasn't you."

He said, "You either!"

He said the whole left side of my face was distorted, and although he tried to get up, something was forcing him down on me. I believed him cause I caught hell trying to lift him off me, and he wasn't that heavy at all. We showered, and that night, I took him home. I felt so scared and didn't know what was going on, but something happened, and it always didn't make sense. We continued to see each other, and suddenly, this sweet man turned into this mentally ill at times lunatic. He would be at my house the night before and run into me at the store and would act like he didn't know me, and when I spoke or attempted to hug him, he would push me away. But the same night expects us to sleep together again. He made absolutely no sense in his actions. He always wanted to have sex, though it was a drug. Every time we made love, it became a weirder experience for me because it seemed like a sex ritual or something.

Every night this man would get in a position of authority, and every night I did not resist him, and it was almost as if I couldn't. He would run from me in the day but, he was right there at night. It made me compare my relationship to my dad's. There was complete turmoil between him and me every day, and it was always on repeat. He was so sweet just two weeks ago and very loving and considerate, and then he flipped And, I had no clue what was going on. Then, he disappeared for a couple of weeks, just out of the blue, and when I found out, he was living in Atlanta. I saw him at his house, and I was shocked to see him because I hadn't heard a thing. I didn't understand why he left, where he was or what was wrong. But, when I saw him, he said he didn't want to deal with me any longer. He kept walking away from me every time I tried to touch him. You would have thought I was trying to poison him with my touch. This rang in my ear like an old sad song. Another man was going to turn on me and couldn't give me an explanation. He

205

said he was going to move to Atlanta to live with his brother. I
kept asking him about us, but he said, "Remember that night we
first made love, the green light, and me and you both looking
different?"

I said, "Yea."

And he said, "I feel that was the devil."

And I looked at him with amazement, and I agreed because
we both grew up in the same church, so we knew the word. We
knew about spirits getting on you because we would watch then
Pastor W cast them out. So, it wasn't anything we didn't know
about spirits. And if he felt the exact way I felt in retrospect. I
knew he understood how I felt under him. He said I want to see
you, but I think you should come here if we do. And that night
was the same as always, but there was no heaviness or weird
feelings at his house. He stayed another two weeks and moved
to Conyers.

I was working on the store side of Blimpy's one night, and I
saw a figure that I knew was Trouble just by the way he walked,
and he came in the store and sped by the register. I went behind
him and thought he would be happy to see me. I walked up to
him and said, "Hey, boo, you home?" He told me to get away
from him. I was like, why?

206

He said, "Just don't touch me."

I stepped back but wanted to know why he was acting that way again since we had just talked the day before. I left him alone that night, I had enough of the back and forth, and it seemed like the relationship bad luck just followed me. I wasn't picking the best candidates either because of my low self-esteem. I just wanted to be loved. I had never been in a situation like this before. I always had someone long-term, even after I divorced my husband. I was always a kept woman. Men always wanted to cuff, so getting a man wasn't a problem. But now It's the trying to get one when you have had hundreds at your feet. That was the headbanger for me. I just could not understand. There had to be a reason for this. Me being unhappy with me wasn't enough; every man had to be unhappy with me as well. In short, I could not have any man and be happy. Just as fast as I got them, I would lose them.

The following day I woke up to a call from my dad accusing me of having a sex offender in his house. I said, "who?"

He said, "Trouble (last name)."

I asked, "Who told you that," but he wouldn't say. I said, "Dad, where did you get that from?"

He said, "Sidechick's daughter."

I repeatedly denied these claims as I knew Trouble and his family and had never heard of him molesting children. Furthermore, Sidechick's daughter doesn't even speak to him. So, I find it hard to believe she stopped my dad and told him about Trouble. I told my dad, "I don't believe it's Sidechick's daughter, and I'm telling you now to tell her to leave me and my business alone."

He kept raising hell at me through the phone, and I got off the phone and went upstairs to his room and said, "Look, I'm not interfering in your life on purpose because I'm trying to have one of my own. And I want no part of what you got going on with this crazy woman."

I didn't want to tell him that trouble and I were done under weird circumstances but, I got so mad at him, declaring how it's his damn house and he didn't want anyone in his house that molested kids. I told him I was not even seeing Trouble anymore; then I shunned him for bringing what that woman was putting down to him, especially about me. She had absolutely no reason to worry about me at all. Yet, she told my dad this foolish mess to start something between us. And I told him I was calling Trouble. And I did and told him what was said about him and who supposedly said it, and he said, "No, that was Sidechick, because she asked me about you the other day."

I even told him all the names my father was calling him and asked if any of them were true. I was more inclined to believe these were lies because of the source. He said, "She was talking about the charges he just had gotten out of prison for, and I had to register as a sex offender because the girl was 16."

I got real upset quickly and asked him to explain.

"Did you have sex with her?"

He refused.

"I was leaving my friend's house, and she was arguing with her boyfriend, and she told him she was gonna walk down the path by herself because she was upset, and they began to fight, and I grabbed him and walked her down the path. It was a bad area, she was young, and I was trying to protect her since he did not care about if she made it home. As we were walking, she stopped, turned around, and walked back toward the house, so he did the same thing, and when he walked her to the driveway, he slapped her on the butt."

I said, "What? Why did you touch her?"

He says, "I don't know."

I said, "Why did you get charged with a sex crime?"

He said, "Because she was 16 but, I have no sex charges on my record, And I can be around kids but, I haven't molested no one, and your dad needs to hear that."

I then went back up to my dad's room and had Trouble on the phone. And he spoke to my dad and said Mr. Crenshaw, Jen told me what was said, and that's not true. I come from a very solid family and would never do anything to harm a child. But my biggest question is why you would listen to a woman you know is crazy and insult my name to Jen or anyone based on the word of someone who doesn't even know me and is crazy. You need to be asking yourself what you're doing in the projects. And why she stabbed her last boyfriend. But don't put dirt on my name, and you don't know if it's true or not, ask me. You wouldn't want that done to your child, so why would you think my mom would want it done to me. If you want me to stay away from your house, I will because I could get in serious trouble if I don't but, don't listen to that woman; she's crazy. And, my dad said, "Well, I never said her name."

Trouble said, "You didn't have to, because she asked me about Jen a few days ago about am I seeing her?"

I thought it was strange but, because she was over at the bootlegger house drinking beer, I guess she felt friendly. But, when I see her again, I'ma says something to her because this is dead wrong, and if someone is going to assassinate my character, it can at least be the truth. But don't do that, Mr. Crenshaw. She was just trying to cause problems between you and Jen. My dad just looked at the phone and said nothing, and I returned downstairs to finish my conversation with Trouble. And, he said that woman has it out for you, and she is trying to cause all kinds of problems for you to try and make your dad put you out. So, she can come back over there, but don't include me, and don't expect me not to defend or stand up for myself. I have paid for what I did.

As I listened to trouble, I still heard that story he told me, and although I didn't judge him, I knew I couldn't even mess around again with him. Since I had already stopped seeing him, that made it even easier to cut the cord. But the nerve of this woman. You have wreaked havoc in my home and what you accused him of wasn't even the case. The next day down to the Sheriff's station, I got a printout of his charges. He was charged with endangering a minor but was still made to register as a sex offender due to the girl was 16. I took the printout to my dad and showed him because, at the end of the day, it mattered to me what he thought about the man I was seeing, but more than anything to prove she was lying on him. And that made me mad as hell. She did this to cause more problems for me with my dad.

She not only was working the witchcraft but would come out of her own home through my dad to torture me and cause more problems in my life. I had absolutely nothing to do with this troll, and she would not leave me alone. She did not pay one bill or even step foot in our home but made it her business to keep stuff going between my dad and me. I was highly upset with my dad for believing this woman. This was the first time she showed me that she wouldn't stop trying to make my life a living hell. She was going to do everything she could to cause problems. I was tired of the lies and defending myself, and it was only getting worse. She started with the bogus charges and knew her statement was false, and she was just trying to get me into trouble.

Since then, she was telling and had my dad believing if I moved, I wouldn't come back to go to court and the infamous I have a criminal record that's why I'm going to prison. But knew nothing about me, yet these are the things she did to get to me. And all were lies. I was so angry that he would come to me and say these things without a shadow of proof, yet he would believe them. It made no sense and made me question my dad. If that day happened again, whose side would he be on my side or hers again?

Reflection: While I'm going through all of this, I am trying to get proof of the character of this woman and show a pattern of the things this woman has to do to other men.

I remember Trouble said that Sidechick had stabbed her previous boyfriend. The guy that cooks at Waffle house in Thomson. I didn't know who they were talking about until I went to waffle house to see him. I was trying to find something to help my case to show this woman was crazy. So, I go up to him and introduce myself, and he says, "I know who you are. What do you want with me."

I said, "I want to talk to you about Sidechick; I'm having some legal problems with her, and I want to know is it true that she stabbed you."

He says, "I don't mean no harm but, I ain't saying nothing else; I don't have, nor do I want to have anything to do with that woman; now have a good day."

After that, he walked away from me so fast, he did not confirm or deny but his walk away was enough for me. I tried to stop him and said, sir, I need your help. Did she stab you?

He went to the back, and I left. I started to go to the husband, but he wouldn't believe me if she was doing what I thought she was doing. But I was on a mission to find someone who knew the truth about this woman. I spoke to a fellow classmate that said everyone in Jewell, Ga, says, "She is crazy as a bed bug. I just want to get the facts that were going to stand in court to show this is a mental basket case who will not leave me alone so they will drop the charges."

We continued that week on the renovation. We still had the porch to be built, and were 15,000 in the hole. I did not know what to do other than potentially get credit cards to help up over the hump until we get the money back. We had filed for a fife warrant for Eduardo since he lived in Gwinnett County. If he approved any work that he did in the state of Ga, we could take the proceeds to go towards the outstanding money he owed us. We hired a lawyer to represent us in the fife case in Gwinnett, and Eduardo showed up and pleaded guilty to the judge and signed an agreement with our lawyer to say that he would pay the money back. He even set up payment arrangements, and the first payment would come in two weeks. What bothered me, though, is he had every opportunity to do this on his own, and if so, why did it have to come to this. He walked over to my dad and me and apologized to us both. I looked at him as if why now; he said my dad is in the hospital, and I am just waiting on him to pass, and I'll get you your money.

After he walked away, I asked my dad didn't it sound as if he was excited about his dad's passing, and dad said, "Yes, but at least now we have an agreement to pay us back the money."

I was so skeptical about the payments at this point but remained hopeful that he would come through and the payments would start in 2 weeks. I had so much on me because I was trying to work at Blimpy's to get the porch built, cabinets were done, and laminate put down correctly since Augustus had left the floor in a mess. Kurt had left money on the table and work not done because he was supposed to put the laminate back down after fixing the kitchen floor. But when he left, the porch or laminate did not get down. I then hired Buster, who was Trouble's uncle, to lay the laminate floor in the kitchen and dining room, and he came and did the job, and this time he argued with dad for taking shortcuts and not connecting the wood properly. Dad told him he did not like the way the flooring looked by the step, and he accused my dad of just not liking him. I am not sure what the spirit was on my dad that day, but he did not like Buster. Come to find out because he also had a thing with Sidechick.

Dad told me from now on, let me know who is working on my house before hiring them. I walked Buster out, trying to calm him down, and he said he didn't have to take that from my dad, that's old news, and he didn't even know he was dating her. But, because dad told her who was doing the floor, she told him about their fling, and dad got jealous or something but, that was the first time I had seen my dad mad at one of the contractors since this all started was wrong. After that blowup, I went back to scheduling people. I then started looking for cabinet installers and someone to build the porch. Dad and I went to the outside store to get some mulch for the flower beds. Because, as I was renovating the inside, I was giving the outside an uplift as well. We met this guy named Suga; when I met Suga, of course, it wasn't dressed like I normally am, I was in tights and a tank top, and I had a hat on because I was doing work all that day and after Buster and my dad argued I really didn't care, I just wanted to get the yard done. As I am talking to Suga, he keeps referring to my dad about how I'm a coin and something

216

else, and how beautiful I was. I often downplayed myself when I was dressed down because I couldn't see what they saw. But, once again, I was just glad someone noticed. The following day, I received a call from Suga saying he hoped he wasn't being inappropriate, but could he ask me to go out on a date with him. I was flattered, but I couldn't see myself going out with him because I didn't date white men. No matter how many white men in my life have ever tried to push more with me or ask me out, I couldn't get past the white/black thing. It was like I always felt if he gets mad at you, he is going to call you the N-word. But I would be his friend, and because he was so sweet and respectful to me, I agreed to go out on a date with him. Why not, I wasn't seeing anyone, and he was a gentleman so, I saw nothing wrong with it. We made a date, went out on a Thursday, and had a really nice time. I guess he was kind of shy due to the age difference and the fact that we were being eyed down by a guy I knew from the '90s when I used to go out to the club. But this guy kept looking at him and me. I got up and went and spoke to him, and he apologized for staring and said, "Jen, I've never seen you with a white guy; why?"

I said, "He seems to be a nice guy. A little older than I'm used to, but a good guy nonetheless. I asked him to stop staring at him as it made him feel uncomfortable."

He laughed and said, "OK, I was just shocked."

I went back to the table and sat down with Suga and told him why my friend was staring, and he made a joke and told him, don't worry, Suga's got it all under control, and we laughed the night away. As I began to talk to Suga more and more and Flowers after flowers and money in only two weeks, Suga was talking about marriage. He knew the situation and was always there to listen to me and lend a helping hand. But lending a helping hand, he wanted more from me. I asked him to help me, and we first built the rose garden. We both got down on our knees and worked until we got it done. I knew that he wanted more because he always brought me the money no matter what I said I wanted. He started spending time at our house off and on and would pop buy and buy things and lay them outside.

I remember going to the stone place on Gordon highway and seeing these two sculptures of two different black kids. One with his hands cupped as if he is holding a flower and the girl was a Lady. She was a girl, but she was posed and poised, and I nicknamed them Sasha and Tito when he took me to the place.

When he laid them on the ground, he left a note, Sasha and Tito. Awe, that was sweet. They were $300 for the set so, I know he really liked me. Suga and I never went farther than a kiss because I just couldn't see it. But that did not stop him from trying. A few weeks went by, and he wanted to see me every day. I couldn't keep doing that with him if I knew it wasn't going to go anywhere. So, I started weaning him off me. I was looking for someone to share what I was going through, and he was a great friend, but I didn't want it to interfere with who I could be with in the future.

So, Dad came home again and said, "Hey, why do you keep having the sex offenders in my damn house."

I said, "What?" Eyes raised, and I said, "Dad, who and what are you talking about now."

He said, "Suga is on the Sex offender list to do the same thing, and this time it's legit."

I didn't know whether to slap my daddy to wake his ass up or curse him out, and both were the wrong thing to do but, he needed a good swift kick in the ass. And, if he is doing what he did before with Trouble, he has really lost his mind because, at this point, he seems to be baiting me and all from misinformation or none of her damn business. Why is this

219

woman still picking at me and messing with me? And is she doing background checks of people I know or visiting the courthouse to get the information on them? Either way, it's becoming an obsession. And it needs to stop. I had never in my life seen such evil mental retardation crap in my life, and for the life of me, I wonder did she know all my dad had to do say was "leave," and I would have been gone. All this wasn't necessary. I didn't need the extra, and either she had a serious vendetta with me or was trying to create problems with the law. Either way, I was watching everything she was trying to do. There was a reason for it. I just needed to keep gathering information.

When I went to Suga about this new information from Sidechick, I really hoped it was not true but, I had to know because I am a mother first, and I have girls and need to make sure they were safe. It really wasn't an issue with me because the relationship was more of a friendship basis, and there was no judgment from me. Some things have explanations but, I wanted to hear his side. He told me that his daughter had accused him of touching her inappropriately, and she told her mom, and he was accused of molestation. He emphatically denied it but was sent to prison for the charge and now is on the sex offender registry because of it. He is waiting to go before the judge to

220

have the sex offender status removed because he has done his time, and it was not true. I told Suga, I am not going to judge you. If you say it did not happen, I believe you but, you must understand how I see things. I have girls, and I know for a fact; I cannot allow them to be around you in any capacity. He told me he understood wholeheartedly but, it was not true.

He also said, "I can't believe this woman is also trying to destroy my reputation to get back at you. If you don't want to see me again, I understand but, this ain't right, Jen."

I understood his claims and agreed that this woman would stop at nothing to make my life miserable. But I still remained his friend because he was good to me. I could not flirt or be around him and had already concluded that prior to me knowing the truth. Therefore, this did not affect our friendship. Things happen, yes, and people lie, but this was an exception for me because it was done out of spite to make me look bad because of who I was dealing with. She again used this man to show my dad the people (men) I was dealing with, and both had sex offender statuses. I didn't know this, but that did not excuse anything. But, due to how it was done, it was not swept under the rug, but it was not used against him either because he was indeed a true friend. My dad changed against Suga, but of course, he was being led by deception and witchcraft, so there was no need to try to explain this situation yet again and no need to argue. I just let it go and continued to add to the list of things this woman was attempting to do to me. Imagine minding your own business just waiting to have your day in court, and the alleged victim is the one who is stalking you to cause problems for you and anyone you see. When will it stop, or will it ever? I didn't know but, I knew that I could never tell my dad of anyone I was dating or even talking to anymore.

Reflection: While I'm going through all of this, I am trying to get proof of the character of this woman and show a pattern of the things this woman has to do to other men. I remember Trouble said that Sidechick had stabbed her previous boyfriend. The guy that cooks at Waffle house in Thomson. I didn't know who they were talking about until I went to waffle house to see him. I was trying to find something to help my case to show this woman was crazy. So, I went up to him and introduced myself, and he said, "I know who you are; what do you want with me."

I said, "I want to talk to you about Sidechick; I'm having some legal problems with her, and I want to know whether it is true that she stabbed you."

He says, "I don't mean no harm but, I ain't saying nothing else, I don't have, neither do I want to have anything to do with that woman, now have a good day." He walked away from me so fast, he did not confirm or deny, but his walk away was enough for me. I tried to stop him and said, "Sir, I need your help. Did she stab you?"

He went to the back, and I left. I started to go to the husband, but he wouldn't believe me if she was doing what I thought she was doing. But I was on a mission to find someone who knew the truth about this woman. I spoke to a fellow classmate who said that everyone in Jewell, Ga, said she was crazy as a bed bug. I just want to get the facts that are going to stand in court to show this is a mental basket case who will not leave me alone so they will drop the charges.

I received a letter from the Public Defenders that said, "Unfortunately, there is a conflict of interest in my case, and they could not represent me."

When I called to inquire about my public defender's status, I was told it was due to the relationship between my dad and the prosecutor. They could not represent me; I said, "Well, how am I supposed to get representation if the officer who is supposed to represent me can't cause my dad is sleeping or slept with this woman."

They said, "A new lawyer will be hired to represent you in our place," and that's when they gave me the name of Lucy Bell. When I contacted Lucy Bell, she told me she would be in contact with me in a few days. When she finally contacted me, she told me that there was a conflict of interest, and she as well could not represent me. She said she represented Sidechick in an insurance case in which I told her I remembered the case because Sidechick was bragging about faking back injury and suing a doctor's office after saying she fell out of a chair. She said to me in confidence I knew she was faking, but it is all over now. I explained she was my second lawyer, and everyone thus far can't help me because of a conflict of interest, so what can I do now, She is sorry you are going through this but, I can't help you and will send you back to the public defender's office, and they will have to help you. I contacted the public defender's office, and they gave me yet another new lawyer Jason Hickman and said he would be contacting me for representation. I asked to speak to the Head public defender, and they refused to talk to me. I didn't understand why my dad sleeping with a public defender caused me to be out of the lawyer. But the Assistant told me she was the one who was going to represent you, and we could not have the victim saying that in court. We are doing what we said and hiring yet another lawyer for you. We must do it this way. I was on my third lawyer, and he called me to set up an appointment with me to come into his office to discuss the case. I explained the case and how I was defending myself against this woman, and he said he would reach out to the DA's office, and he did by email and told her that I had a very strong case for self-defense.

The following week I went in for my appointment, and when I walked in the door, I inquired about what I had told him and the email he sent. He told me he had spoken to the Assistant District attorney even after sending the email to suggest I could win my case in self-defense, and there were no offers at the time. He said, "The only offer is that I would serve the time consecutively."

These people were trying to give me 50 years. There was no way I would plead guilty to these charges. This was a no-brainer. And I declined. He then began to speak on myself and the way I carried myself and how I spoke so eloquently that he felt I would be able to convince a jury of anything and that he was running for DA of Augusta Ga and how he may be able to use this case as an example of how victims are being treated unfairly and asked if I would be in one of his commercials.

I said, "Sure, why not?"

We met with his assistant, and she agreed. I told him what was going on with the witchcraft, and his assistant was intrigued but, said you may not want to mention that because it's taboo, and we don't want to scare anyone away. Just stick to the facts. And, I said, how can I not mention the facts?

She said, "You can but not those facts," and we scheduled to shoot the commercial the following Monday, and then Covid hit, and the world went on lockdown; people were scared and losing their lives quickly, and no one knew how to stop it. I had never seen something like this before, I was truly scared, and then I was watching the news and wondered how long it would take me to go to court, and then My lawyer was on TV, and he was the first Lawyer in Augusta to contract Covid. He was sitting on the sidewalk at Augusta University, having a hard time breathing, and it seemed like no one wanted to go near him. I was worried about the man because he had met me and may have been exposed to evil.

At this point, I discounted nothing that was happening with this case, with my lawyers, and with now Covid. But I was also

226

honestly worried about my case too and what would happen. Would it be years now? Would I be on lawyer number 4? What was next for me? After three weeks, I got a call from Mr. Hickman, I inquired about his health, and he said he was ok and still recovering and did not want me to come into the office because of it. I told him I appreciated that, but he wanted to update me on my case. He had received the discovery information for my case, and he asked me if I was on drugs that day? I said I smoke marijuana but, I don't consider that to be a drug. He said the way you were acting that day seemed as if you were on drugs and having a drug-related episode. I denied smoking that day and said this was more than just drugs, sir. I blanked out and did not know what had happened. He then said, "I am going to send the video of the dash cam and let you review." He said, "call me when you receive it."

I got the disk the next day and watched it on my laptop. All I could say was, Lord, what happened to me that day? I don't remember saying or doing anything but, it seemed as if I was a raging volcano, and I wouldn't stop until they put me in the back seat of that car. I had lost control of my actions and my mind. I seemed as if I was possessed, and there was no other way to explain it. He said, you can plead guilty, and I'm sure the

227

judge would be lenient with you since you do not have a criminal record, but I am not sure. I was so ready to get this over with and so tired of going through all of this, I just wanted to accept my responsibility and be done with it. My lawyer Mr. Hickman contacted the district attorney and scheduled me to go before the judge the following Monday. On Sunday afternoon, I received a call from Mr. Hickman's secretary telling me Mr. Hickman was placed back in the hospital after having a problem breathing due to Covid complications, and she was not sure when he would be back to work.

She said, "We have canceled your court appointment and will contact you when Mr. Hickman is ready to appear."

I took this as a sign that I wasn't doing the right thing. I continued on and was prepared for when it was my time to go to court.

I continued to work at Blimpy's, and then one day, a childhood friend came in the store named Meyer. He lived around the road from me, and he and my dad were gambling partners, and I considered him a friend. At least until that day. I was still in training and saw him, and a guy watched me talk to Blimpy. We were standing kind of close and because he was showing me how to run the register and as I looked over the register. I saw the guy watching me and whispering to the other guy. I spoke and waited on him, and he left. A few minutes later, he came back in and confronted Blimpy about him not caring about the black community, and they exchanged words, and he left.

At the time, I was friends with this guy, and I looked on his Facebook page, and he was going in on Blimpy. About how he didn't like blacks, and we were the primary source of his income. I said OKAY, thanks for letting me know. But then he started talking about how he was sleeping with his employees for jobs, and I said, "Hold up, wait a minute."

And everyone started commenting that they knew who he was talking about, and I said, wait, is he talking about me? But then someone said she no longer worked there, and I sighed. But then Meyer said, well, he got another working now, and she will be his next one. Now, I knew he was talking about me. And that pissed me off because, as hard as it was for me to get a job, I didn't want to be labeled as one of Blimpy's girls. I already felt debilitated having to work for 8.00 an hour and clean floors and toilets. I was beyond depressed about my circumstance, but I ate it and kept on working.

All that day, I watched Blimpy and how angry he was at the posts that Meyer continued to make about him, and he responded he was so upset. I wondered if there was no truth why he was so bothered? Then Blimpy made the tragic mistake of looking at my print through my pants and I saw the truth in his eyes. After another woman visited Blimpy who was not his wife, and they went in the back room for a very long time leaving me alone to run the store and I still wasn't trained and not coming out to assist me when I called him. I decided that night that this was not the job for me and quit. I was not going to be anyone's piece just to have a job, and I felt very uncomfortable about the things that were being said about Blimpy. But, when he looked between my legs, it was inappropriate enough for me to know there was some truth to what Meyer said about Blimpy. And, although Meyer was telling the truth, there could have been a way to tell it without including me in his post, especially since there was never anything inappropriate until that day. I quit after my shift, never to return to that store again. I had to find a job but decided to take a quick break to do more work on the house. We were so behind due to the lack of money. We got approved for a Home Depot card which helped with the materials but, we were still short on the money side due to the $15000 we were missing that Eduardo and Augustus had taken. I had about $13000 to work with and still had to get the cabinets, siding, windows, roof, and porch, the electrician paid, and the garage doors. There was no way without the extra funds we lost that we were going to be able to do it. I started maneuvering and got the cabinets and countertop for the kitchen ordered with the Home Depot card. My list started getting smaller when I met Slim.

When I met and hired slim, I heard so many good things about Slim and the type of work he did when building houses. I was often told to go look at the house he had built. On the day I met him at his house, I was amazed because it was a mansion like I had never seen before. We agreed that he would not receive any money until the job was done, and based on what I was hearing, I really thought this time God would shine on me and not allow me to go through any more turmoil with this house and my dad and these shady grady contractors. But guess it was too much to ask for because the next two contractors to come were destined to be the third contractors I would have to take to court.

On the first day I met Slim, he tried to ask a lot of personal questions about me, and I was very limited and watchful of telling him anything. I didn't know him that well only his name, and I wasn't going to be friendly on purpose, just so they would know who they were dealing with and not try to play me. When Slim reached out to touch me on the first day, I cursed him out and told him, if you touched me again, I would fire you.

He proceeded to say to his partner, we have a feisty one here, and they laughed. His partner was an old man who had built houses for over 30 years, and I really didn't understand how he could assist him because the man could not see. They began building the gable porch that I wanted for so long and had waited almost a year to be built due to all the mishaps and problems with all the contractors who had come and gone. They not only built the trusses but had the porch frame built in one day. I was so excited because although we started wrong, I finally had someone that put in the work and did what I asked without hesitation. Slim came to work the following day, and I asked them to lower the porch frame because it was too high. Immediately Slim became upset, I brushed it off and went on about my business, and he lowered it with no problems. We were told there was still more work that needed to be done for the garage to pass inspection, and Slim said, "He could fix that too."

I was like, "ok, we are going to get this done."

And then the real Slim showed up. On the following morning, his partner Mr. Alph showed up alone. I asked how he could work if he couldn't see, and he stated that he had been doing this for 30 years, so he knew where things went. I was so skeptical because why would you leave a blind man to work alone? This man could only see maybe 20% of the time. There was no way he could do work that required measuring and cutting. Included in fixing the garage and getting it ready for inspection, Mr. Alph tasked himself with cutting out the back garage door.

I said, "How in the world are you going to see how to cut the door out? Where is Slim?"

He said, "He told me he had a doctor's appointment."

I called Slim, and at first, he didn't answer my calls. But, called back and said he was on the way. It was 9 am. Slim came to work around 2 pm. I explained to him that if you are hired to do a job, you need to be present or call me and let me know you are not coming. The renovation had taken so much of my life with these contractors not showing up, taking off when they wanted too and not caring if I had plans or things to do, and Slim was proving to me just as bad as the others. After that day, he did the repeated no-call no-show for the remainder of the week, and when he did show up, he seemed like he was under the influence of something and smelled like a liquor cabinet. I said Slim. I don't know what's going on with you but, I need this porch finished, and the things I asked that were extra, and we will not get anywhere like this. Of course, my dad could no longer resist and came out one day after finally allowing me to handle this contractor and began to converse with Mr. Alph. I knew it would be a problem when I was talking to Slim about his drinking and not coming to work, and My dad said Jennifer, let the man work. I respectfully said, I am, and Slim started talking to my dad about how I don't play, and then he proceeded to say, how would you like me to be your Son In law. My dad just laughed and said, I don't have anything to do with it. That is totally between you and her. And Slim started laughing and tried to grab me and hug me. I told him for the last time do not to touch me.

On a regular job, you would be fired, and if you try that again, you will be fired here too. I don't know what in the hell makes you think you can just touch on women. This is not a game. He said, Jenny, why you so mean. I said, first off, don't call me Jenny, and second why would you think I want you touching me? My dad didn't say a word. He asked my dad why I was so mean. I waited for my dad to defend me, and he made a joke out of it instead. I was highly amazed because my dad would never let anyone disrespect me, yet he stood there and saw this guy try to hug me, and he was right there and didn't say a word. I realized I was on my own, and I went inside for the remainder of the day because I had nothing else to say. Since he was so accepting and buddy buddy with the contractor, my dad was there. I let him handle it. Slim and Mr. Alph finished the porch on that day, and the only thing left was the indoor-outdoor carpet and the railing for the porch. The door to the back garage door was complete and all the other things needed to pass inspection, and the garage doors were ready to go. And, then it happened on the following morning, I went over to the outside store to get some more mulch from Suga for the rose garden, and he told me that Slim had been over there picking up a lawnmower and asked him isn't he dating me? He said no, she is my friend.

He said, "Good because she is going to be my wife, and I don't want to have to fight you about her."

He says, "She acts strange, doesn't she?"

He said, "I don't know what you are talking about."

He said, "She just acts strange to me, don't want nobody to touch her and like she is more than anyone else."

When, he told me this, I said, "Oh yeah, really. Strange... let's see how strange I act when I get back to the house."

Suga said, "I believe he is on drugs, so be careful, ain't no telling what he will do."

My Dad, Slim, and Mr. Alph were standing up in the garage while Slim was working on the trim on for the garage doors, and I said Slim, I act strange?

He said, "What are you talking about, Jenny?"

I said, "Don't call me Jenny, but who are you to ask Suga about him and me, then proceed to tell him you are going to marry me when you are just a worker. How dare you speak on my name and ask any man about me. Then you say I act strange if you don't get this job done and get out of my house today. You will not be paid. I have had it with your lax work ethic, just showing up when you want to, and now you are talking about me to other men, in particular a man who is my friend, and telling him, you don't want to have to fight him over me. Have you lost your mind?"

Mr. Alph stood up and said, "You know what? I am so tired of you. All you do is bitch and complain about every damn thing, and I'm sick of you, and you are right, we need to get this job done before I say something I shouldn't to you because once again, I'm sick of your shit."

I stood back and looked at Mr. Alph and said, was I talking to you. He said no, but I'm talking to you. I looked at my dad, and he turned his back and walked into the house. I said, "Dad, will you let him talk to me like that?" He kept walking. Mr. Alph then said, "You are causing all these problems with the workers. No wonder you can't keep nobody to work."

I said, "Oh yeah, where did you get that from?"

And then he said, "Causing all kinds of problems with your dad and his woman, when are you going to shut your mouth and stop causing problems?" Then he said, "And look at how much money you have caused your daddy to lose!"

I said, "Mr. Alph, first off, you don't know nothing about me, and since you want to listen to my dad, ask him why there were so many problems, and you have no idea what kind of hell that woman has caused around here, but, since you want to run your mouth about things you have no idea about and ask my dad where the money is and who lost it? And, when you get all the correct answers, you can leave and don't come back. I have tried to respect you since you are my elder, and my problem was with

Slim and running his mouth but, since you want to attempt to disrespect me, you can leave."

Slim said, "No, we are going to get this job done today, so we both can leave."

I said, "That would be your best thing before you leave without getting paid because I'm not the one to play with, and both of you are out of line."

And then I went upstairs for my dad and laid into him. I asked how you have the audacity to be talking about me to the workers. Haven't you caused enough problems with the workers and corrected me and changed up on me in front of them to the point where now, you're having conversations with them and accusing me of causing problems in your relationship. How dare you! Did you tell them about all this woman has done to you and me? Did you show them your furniture while you out there painting this rosy picture of her and slandering me? And how could you blame me for losing the money when it was you, dad. We are on hold now because of you, and you want to blame me? The nerve of you. How could you, dad?

He said, "Jennifer, when this is all over with, I'ma tell you about yourself."

238

I said, "Dad, please don't wait, let's get this out now because you left me out that to be harassed by a man who went to another man and talked about me, who keeps trying to touch me inappropriately, and now his partner is insulting me based on the lies you are telling them and you sitting up here in the room like it doesn't matter. What is wrong Dad, what happened to you? Are you so rooted up that you can't see when your daughter needs you? Instead, all you want to do is point fingers at me and blame me for your problems. I am tired of this, all of this, and I see now I am really on my own but, you better get down there because you are about to have a serious problem if I go back out there today."

My dad got up, looked me in my eyes, and rolled them, and walked down the steps to go back out to the garage. I was so done with my dad and what bothered me so much was that at every turn, with every person, my dad betrayed me and saw my dad for who he really was on that day. There was no second-guessing. He did not care how I looked to anyone if he was made out to be the good guy. The dad I knew would never do this to me, and the fact that he knew he was wrong and didn't care, didn't make me feel good at all about my father.

I realized that I could not trust him. I had a very uneasy feeling, and I got in my car and left that day and stayed gone till late that night to avoid him because I did not want to deal with or see him. I would have cursed him out, and I didn't care anymore. After Slim and Mr. Alph finished the covering of the indoor-outdoor carpet and the railing and columns on the porch, my dad paid them, and they left, and I never saw either of them again. Well, I did see Mr. Alph at the store, but he didn't know who I was because he couldn't really see me. But I thought if he couldn't see me, how could he drive? I laughed but was glad to get rid of that team. And, without having to sue them was a blessing but, there still was a major problem between dad and me, and I knew it was time for me to make a move but, I didn't know how I was going to do it. Since I had just quit my job, I knew I needed to find income. I applied for this other job as an insurance agent; I went through the training course and all, and when they told me I had to do a background check, I knew that would be my last day. I got the same call from the Insurance agency HR Department, and they told me I did not clear the background check due to pending charges on my record. I absolutely lost it. I cried, screamed, kicked and screamed, and said, what have I done to myself. This job was a salary job making upwards of 60,000 a year, and I just lost it before I even got started. This was the second job I had lost due to pending charges in two months. There was nothing I could do. I was in a stronghold until I went to court, and there was nothing I could do. I felt like this woman had destroyed my life, and with the continuous things she was trying to do to me concerning my father, I didn't know how much I could take. I just didn't know. I was six months in and couldn't get a job making more than $8.00, and that wasn't even enough to pay my car payment out of one check. I couldn't live this way. I just didn't know what to do. How am I supposed to live? I thought as I scheduled the siding and roof people.

I was now working with a little over $7000 and had no idea how I was going to get the roof, the siding; the electrician paid out of what I had left with no help or suggestions or solutions from dad at all. I called Southern siding and inquired about the siding and the windows to stretch the money. I asked if they financed, and they said yes. I then told dad, and he made a contract to get the windows and siding done. The crew that came out was nice at first but, we all know that wouldn't last long. The supervisor got upset about the work that was done on the porch and how it was uneven. I wondered why every contractor that came complained about the other contractor. This was also a thing that I endured when trying to explain what the previous person did right or wrong, and it was always wrong, and they were always gone or left, or we argued, or they did half-ass work, and I was always the one caught in the crossfire. My dad never got involved. Just sat back and let me argue with them, and then he would jump in and take their side, and this was no different. When I was trying to explain what Slim and Mr. Alph did, the supervisor told me, "Let me talk to your dad; he knows what I'm talking about."

I said, "Oh, ok, you can talk to him but, he is going to direct you right back to me because I'm the one who has been involved since day one and can tell you more about this house than he ever could, but you go ahead and talk to them," and once again I walked inside. It just didn't make any sense.

And what also didn't make any sense is every time, my dad just sat on the sideline listening and waiting for something to happen as if he was not involved. But when or if something did happen and I stood up for myself, he would go against me. And try and smooth it out with the contractor. It just didn't make sense at all. I was done shaking my head, screaming, cursing, storming off to my room. Either he was going to get involved and take responsibility, or we were going to end the work that day and what did he do. He did just as I said, "Dad sent the siding supervisor right back over to me to explain what was done and how by Slim and Mr. Alph. He looked really cheap, walking back over to me, and I didn't say a word and told him what he needed to know." The siding came out beautiful until we realized the siding up top on my dad's part and the bottom siding did not match, and they had to take all of the sidings off of the front that they had just spent all day putting up. I suggested wouldn't it be easier just to do the top over. They said no because that would be more work, and then we had to wait a few days to get the new order in with the right color of siding.

During that time, I had reached out to a cabinet installer named wormy. The show must go on right, and he agreed to install the cabinets for $1200.00. I just wanted to get the cabinets out of the living room. They had been sitting there for almost four months since Augustus left, and he had also promised to hang the cabinets but, we all know how that went, and now I needed them to put up in the kitchen. When the cabinet installer came to our house, he noticed an air vent that would be covered if he put the cabinets on the wall. For some reason, when the house was built, the air vent was placed on the side of the wall in the kitchen, and if covered, there would be no air ventilation in the kitchen. Therefore, I had to hire a heating and ac installer to move the vent and delay the installation of the cabinets another week. Now, this one, let's call him pearly. Pearly was different; most of the contractors got mad with me after they began to work for whatever reason that made no sense. But pearly got out of the truck with the biggest attitude the first and the second time. He got mad because he had to drive from North Augusta and could not install the cabinets because of the air vent, and then got mad the second time because I refused to pay him a travel fee for coming back the second time since I wasn't ready the first time. No, I can't make this up. He tried to charge me $60.00 additionally for a travel fee, and after I said, "I don't think that was fair and after he had put up all the cabinets."

He started cursing at me for not wanting to pay the fee. And, then I had picked out handles for the drawers from his store in which he told me he would charge me $5.00 a handle, he then raised his price to $10.00 And, when I said that is not what you told me in the store, he lost it and had the biggest break down I had ever seen and for what? He started cursing and packing up his stuff and calling me all kinds of bitches and telling me I couldn't afford his stuff, and I looked at him and said, what is wrong with you? If I couldn't afford your prices, why would I agree to pay you 1200.00, of which I have already paid half as a deposit? Why are you cursing and yelling at me, and I wasn't the one who misquoted? You did, so chill out. He kept on cursing and told his worker lets to get out of here something was wrong with this lady. I said, oh no, you are not going to be cursing at me for something I didn't do. This is all on you. He told me, "You can keep the $600.00 you owe me. I'm not finishing the job," and left.

My dad came downstairs and said, "What is going on?"

I explained that this guy just lost it over the price of the handles changing and tried to charge me a $60.00 travel fee, and I refused, and he cursed me out and called me all kinds of bitches over some handles for the cabinets. And as Pearly was getting in the van and putting his stuff in the van, my dad came down and said, "What did you do, now?"

I rolled my eyes at him and told him what happened, and Pearly was still cursing me out and said, "Suck my dick bitch, and grabbed his little package."

At that moment, I just started hysterically laughing at him and said, "You know that's too small for grabbing right," and turned to my dad and said all over some handle's dad and a travel fee. He left the money we owed him. He said, "He left the money."

I said, "Yes, and he said something was wrong with me and left the money."

Because I would pay the extra money, I continued to laugh at that foolishness and knew there was something so funny going on here in this house it was sad. Anytime I was involved, and it involved this house, there was conflict. It took me to almost the last three contractors to do jobs to realize that whatever was being done to me somehow included the house. The way dad was acting, the fact that there have been at least over 20 contractors to work on this house. I had a problem with every one of them, and honestly, most of them, either they were slacking and doing just what I was accusing them of, or dad was talking about them to me. They felt they could disrespect me, but this joker pearly was something special, even after he and his worker George left.

I tried to call George, offer him the job, and pay him the remainder to finish the cabinets and put the crown molding around them. Pearly grabbed the phone and told me if I called him again, he was going to put a warrant on me for harassment. I fell out laughing again because this craziness further confirmed what I just said about the house and let me know it ain't over yet, but he didn't want to let his worker make money over some handles and a travel fee. This was the ultimate eye-opener. All this stress and argument after argument with these contractors, my coworkers, Trouble, and person after person.

Anyone who came in contact with me in this house it seemed like a bad spirit got on them, and in return, It got on me because I spent more time defending myself than a little bit. And did not know why, for God's sake. Why? But now I knew, and I began searching again. This time the entire house to find what was put down, but all it left me was tired.   Oh my God, It's the house. This woman cleaned our house for years, so I'm sure she would not just lay it down where we could see it. I began searching the vents and even the crawl spaces while thinking. Everyone seems to change when they are talking or dealing with me at this house. I also had to think that it was so bad people were even leaving money behind. There has to be a hell storm brewing over the house to cause all of this turmoil between my dad and me and me and everyone who came to do work here. I tried to say I saw through them that's why they popped off at me, but I honestly started off very nice to all of them, and when they changed and started slacking or changed for absolutely nothing at all and wanted to argue, I was ready for them. But ever since I came home, there has been turmoil. I went to jail from our HOUSE, every contractor argued with me at our HOUSE, and every time I got into it with my dad, and he turned on me, it was at our HOUSE! And, I had to find it, but no matter how hard I looked and asked God to show me. I could never find what was wreaking havoc in our home.

At, that point there were now two contractors who left money to not deal with the house or me, and I was glad because we needed the money but skeptical as to what was next because I hadn't found anything in any wall or under the house or even in the closets. I searched all over the house, including my dad's room, and found nothing. I kept thinking about how I did nothing to this man but quoted him on the price he gave me and refused to pay a travel fee, and I got treated like that.

At one point, I hesitated, and I was scared to even go to the next step of getting the metal roof installed, but I was not going to let the spirit in the house win. I was going to continue to fight. I was not going to let this evil witch defeat me because she designed this and hid it very well if she couldn't put the horrible musty musk on the walls. She was going to make sure she had something down to replace it. And made sure I couldn't smell it because she knew I would be looking for it. She was not going to win, and that was the end of that. After, I had to pay the electrician Mr. Goolsby most of his money for wiring the inside and outside of the garage, the metal roof, and Tsuanami for painting the entire inside of the bottom level and the new garage. Also, I had bought materials for the roof. I also had to pay the deposit of $1000 to order the garage doors that left me with about $500. We still had to pay for the windows we ordered, which was about $7500, and pay the balance owed for the garage doors and the remaining balance for the electrician, and we were out of money. We needed $10,000 at least to finish this job. Everything was already in play, either halfway installed or ordered, so we had no choice but to complete it. If we didn't pay the balance on the Garage doors, the paint would get damaged because there were no doors, just a piece of plastic on each door. I went to my dad and said Dad, we don't have enough money to pay for the windows, the garage doors, and Mr. Goolsby, what are we going to do?

My dad looked at me and said, "No, what are you going to do. Cause, I don't have any money, and I ain't borrowing any money from nobody. You figure it out."

I said, "What? Dad. What are you saying?" And quickly reminded him if it wasn't for him, we would have the money we need, and this ain't my mess to fix and left out of the room flaming and down to my last try. I could not believe that my dad caused us to lose almost 16,000 and now holds no responsibility for replacing it. I was so angry about my dad I left as I was riding, and I called Suga. And told him what was going on. He and I were still friends, not as close as before due to what was told, but he listened and was there to help if I needed him.

For anything, and I appreciated him for that. He knew there could never be anything between us because of his record, but a friend, he was true because I was going through a lot, and I just needed someone to listen with no intention but to be there. And he was that guy. And I appreciated him for it. I was constantly speaking to him about the renovation. How we lost 16 thousand dollars, and when I told him what happened that day when I told my dad I was out of money. He told me it was my problem and I'm not the one responsible, and how upset I was he looked and me, and he said,

"Jen, I'ma help you out, I know you want to get this house done, and you have endured enough. And I'm going to speak to

Mama and see if we can help replace most of the money that you lost."

I looked at the phone and said, "WHAT!?"

He said, "How much do you need right now to get this house finished and get you out of this mess."

I hesitated, looked up to the sky, and said I don't know at least $10,000. He told Jen when that evil woman tried to hurt you by telling your dad that stuff about me; I know it bothered you a lot but, the one thing that you did not do was judge me, you listened to me and said that although we could never have a relationship, we still could remain friends that touched my heart because every woman that has ever found out about why I went to prison has tried to get as far away from possible from me.

They automatically assumed I did it. But you asked me, and when I told you I didn't do it, you didn't change on me. We are not as close as we were, but I can still call you anytime and appreciate your friendship. We have some money saved up, and I want to help you. Give me until in the morning, and I will let you know how long it will take to get it to you. Would you believe my first thought was I going to have to sleep with him now? There was no way this man was going to give me $10,000 to finish our house and not expect anything in return. Do not get me wrong, Suga was a bowlegged sexy walking man. My prejudice got in the way at first concerning his race And, then the charge against him was such a turn-off for me that if I had to sleep with him for the money, I honestly would have turned it down. I was a molestation victim when I was young. Therefore, I couldn't do it, and if he made that a condition, our house may have stayed unfinished as far as I'm concerned, it was not my responsibility to come up with the money anyway, so I wasn't prepared to go against my beliefs for any man. But then he said and didn't worry about it; we will work out something. I said something like what, still in shock. He said, "How to pay me back."

I said, "Suga if you do this, I will pay you back every dime."

He said, "I'll call you in the morning."

The following morning like clockwork Suga called me on his way to work and said I talked to Mama, and she said OK! His mama is 96 years old, and he cares for her at home, and I only met her one time. She was a very sweet lady who liked to make crochet Angels, and the first time I met her, she gave me an angel and said, "You will be blessed!"

Little did I know that she would be the one to bless me. Suga said, "We will call a lawyer to draw up the paperwork. Are you sure you can pay it back?"

I said, "I would not have it any other way. I am still in shock and cannot believe that you would do this to help us finish our house but, I am grateful and will pay you back what I owe you. I promise. We scheduled to meet the following day at this lawyer's office, and Suga had typed up a loan contract to be signed by him and his mama and myself. I always read over contracts before I signed them, and this was no different.

As, I got to the last page, it stated in the event that Suga and I became married, my loan would be paid in full. I said, "Hold up, showed him the paper, and said, why is this in the contract? We are not going to get married."

He said, "I'm sorry, this was the first copy I printed. I will take it out if it makes you feel uncomfortable."

I said, "Yes, please, because you never mentioned this to me before when we were talking about this, and why would you put this in the contract anyway? You know how I feel about us, we are friends, and that's all we will ever be. If you are doing this to get me to marry you or sleep with you, please keep your money because I can't be bought."

When he marked through the part, I was speaking of and signed his initials on the voided page. He and his mama signed the paperwork, and all that was left was my signature. I looked at his mama, and she said, go ahead, baby, we are going to help you. And, Suga was just trying some mess. He didn't mean no harm. I took a deep breath and signed the paperwork. He then had it notarized, and then he handed me a check for $10,000. I tried to compose myself but, I was crying elephant tears. I could not believe this man cared about me this much that he went into his savings and pulled out $10,000 for me.

For the first time in a long time, I knew my worth. I didn't sell my soul or my body, and I stood firm, changing the wording in the contract before I signed anything, and he still gave me the money. Out of all I had been through, someone believed the story I was telling them and was able to help me replace money that I didn't lose. After thanking Suga and his mama repeatedly and gratefully, I left the lawyer's office and went to the bank and cashed the check. I just sat in the car and stared at the $10,000 laying all over the seat and said, "Now, we can get the house finished finally."

I thanked God and went home to tell my dad. He could not believe it. He asked me what I did for it, and I said I was his friend. He said, do you have to pay it back and I said I wouldn't have it any other way.

He said, "You have got to be crazy to think this man gave you $10,000 and doesn't want anything in return."

I said, "He does."

"What's that?"

I said, "He wants his money back, and I signed an agreement to say that is what I am going to do, and now we have the money to finish the house. We can both split the payment and pay him back every month."

Dad said, "No, you are going to pay him back cause I ain't got no money. I looked at my dad and said, "Do you honestly think I will pay this man back all of this money by myself when I didn't cause us to be in the hole? I am trying to help you out because you are the one who gave away the money, not me. And right now, you are being very ungrateful and telling me you are going to make me pay all of the money back; Daddy, you must think I'm a fool."

He said, "I don't know what you are but, I know if you took the money from the man, you need to give him the money back. I am not paying no more money for this house, especially since I didn't tell you to do all of this to this house."

I said, "Dad, you didn't go get materials? Didn't you write checks to people who did the work? You didn't sit downstairs or outside with Eduardo and Augustus and talk to them about what they were doing? So, you didn't tell me to all of this to this house but agreed to all of that. Are you ok?"

He said, "All I asked for was a simple house, but, no, you wanted to turn it into your house."

I said, "Dad, didn't you tell me to do the house the way I wanted to, so why are you acting like I did something wrong?

Why Dad, "He said, you went overboard, so you figured out a way to pay the man.

I said, "You know what, dad, what I'm going to do is pay myself, and I'm going to take this $10,000, and I'm going to do with it what I should have been done and get the hell out of your house. Because I finally see that you don't care about any of the stress you have caused me. You have betrayed me at every cost and been against me, and all I have ever tried to do was help you. I am sick of your mess."

I finally realized I didn't have to take it and left my dad standing in the middle of the floor, looking dumbfounded. I went downstairs and began looking for my nephew and me a place to stay. Fortunately, the first townhouse I looked at was for rent on Facebook. And I really liked the fact that it had bathrooms in the bedrooms, so I sent a message and received a response instantly. The person acted as though they knew me just by the way they said, "Hi, how are you."

I asked who they were, and she said, "Ok, when do you want to move in?"

I said, "As soon as possible."

She said, "When can you come and sign your lease. I was like, this is way too easy. Is this a scam?"

She said, "Ok, I can meet you tomorrow, and on the following day at 1 pm, I pulled up to the Food Lion in Grovetown and it got out of my car, and it was my classmate from high school."

She said, "You didn't know it was me, but I knew who you were and knew you would do right by me. That is why I told you to come on and sign your lease."

All I could say was look at God. He knew it was time to get me out of this mess. I then paid my security deposit and first month's rent. She told me the lights and water were still in the previous tenant's name, and the order had been placed for that Friday. She asked when I wanted to move in, and I said honestly today, but I can wait till tomorrow because I still have to get a truck.

She said, "OK, and gave me my keys." I went back home and started packing as I walked to the car to take things to put in the car. My dad came downstairs, looked at me, and said, "What are you doing?"

I said, "I'm getting out of your house and letting you figure out how to come up with the money because I am officially done."

He said, "Where are you going? I told you that you couldn't leave because I will lose my house if you don't go to court."

And I said, "Dad and I told you to stop listening to dumb people; why wouldn't I go to court? Don't I have just as much to lose if I don't? And why would you let some women convince you that I wouldn't mind when I'm your child. There is no way anyone can tell me about my child, especially when they are my child's enemy. What happens to you, Dad."

I said, "Dad, you have got to get it together," and suddenly, I heard my dad in a voice that wasn't his but sounded like a woman saying, "All y'all got is a big house with no money."

And, all I heard and saw was Sidechick saying it through my dad, and I looked at him and didn't even respond. I just walked away and shook my head. As hard as I worked on that house, my dad just slapped me in the face with it and accused us of being broke in the process based on what Sidechick said, "And I wasn't even trying to acknowledge anything that said."

I asked myself why my dad would say that if it had not been said to him? It was his house because it didn't make sense for him to say those words. So, it had to be her words either way; that was my queue. It was time for me too and to get far away as possible from my dad because now this woman had convinced him that he didn't deserve a nice big home. The very home he asked me for over a year ago, and now he feels he doesn't deserve the house of his dreams. He deserves to live in the projects. Om the following morning, I incorporated and paid three people $300.00, and I had all my things in a Uhaul truck within 3 hours, and I left my dad's house on that day.

As, I was leaving out the door, my dad said, I can't believe you are going to take the money and run and leave me with all of this debt.

I said, "Dad, I gave you a chance to agree to pay the money back, and you said no. And that was the last time you were going to betray me now since you listen so much to Sidechick ask her to give you the money to help you finish this house. Good luck with that!"

With tears in my eyes, I left my dad standing on the porch that day, and I moved to my new townhouse and finally into my peace.

To be Continued...

THE DAY MY DAD CAME HOME

VOLUME

TWO

WILL BE RELEASED JANUARY 22,2023

JENNIFER CRENSHAW

Made in the USA
Columbia, SC
14 May 2022

60405689R00150